The Nonprofit Buyer

Strategies for Success from a Nonprofit Technology Sales Veteran

Andrew Urban

Copyright © 2010 by William Andrew Urban
All Rights Reserved
All corporate names and logos mentioned are the sole property of
the owners and no rights or titles are inferred here within.

Edited by Lori Hood Lawson

- Dei gratia -

To my wife, Jill, for her constant love and support.
To my girls, Anne and Rebekah, the best daughters in the whole world, for always believing in their daddy.

Table of Contents

Chapter	Page
Preface	7
Chapter 1: Why This Matters	9
Chapter 2: The Nonprofit Buyer	29
Chapter 3: Unreliable Buying Techniques	47
Chapter 4: The Other Side of the Fence	67
Chapter 5: How a Sales Process Works on You	87
Chapter 6: Sales 101	101
Chapter 7: The Nonprofit Buyer Model of Control	117
Chapter 8: Adapting to Your Organization	149
Chapter 9: Closing the Sale	159
Chapter 10: Deal done! On to the Next One...	163
Notes	193

Preface

The Nonprofit Buyer is a message I have wanted to put into words for a number of years. I have been told by more than a few they wish this book had been written years ago to help them in their work. It is the culmination of many phone calls, meetings, conversations, triumphs, and disappointments. It is also the combination of two very different worlds I have balanced in between for most of my life.

Growing up around, working in, and being a part of the various organizations I have in my life means so much to me. After college, my career took me on a high tech sales path that finally, as if meant to be, merged my passion with my professional training over ten years ago. As someone of both worlds I have tried to find ways to bring the two together to the benefit of both. The Nonprofit Buyer is my attempt to bridge the divide between technology and its application for the betterment of a nonprofit mission, between a vendor and a nonprofit, between a sales representative and you in your everyday work at your organization. The concepts in this book are universal and are not solely useful in technology situations, but as this is my area of expertise it is the brush with which I choose to paint.

A Nonprofit Buyer is:

- ☑ A person who can, with confidence, take control of their own buying processes
- ☑ A team who, with unity in purpose, can communicate its needs to the world
- ☑ An organization who knows, with assurance, what they are buying will have the greatest impact possible on the mission

The past few years have seen an ever-increasing amount of pressure to provide more services with potentially less available revenue while still having to be more accountable and transparent than ever. The desire to reach out to new donors, do more with current donors, and provide the openness funders and donors expect today has been a challenge for all. The technology most organizations have turned to in order to solve these pains has not always been the hoped-for cure. I know we are always told technology will, Jetsons-like, make our life simpler and easier, but it just isn't always the case. Is it your organizations fault? Is it the vendors fault? Is the software doing what it should? Is the hardware breaking down? The answer is never a simple yes.

In The Nonprofit Buyer you will learn to see yourself in a new light, understand those who serve the nonprofit community better than ever, and gain a model of control that will enable your organization to be a buyer instead of one that is being sold to.

I will be the first to admit there are portions of this book you may already know. However, I guarantee there will be sections you will be excited to read and learn from. The hardest parts will be those areas that may be uncomfortable for you as I discuss a number of ineffective buying techniques that have become ingrained as standard modes of business, but truly need to change. It's time to find a new path. It's time to create a more balanced relationship between vendor and nonprofit that focuses on the impact to, or rather, the Return on Mission that can be found if we all share a common goal.

I'm excited to begin this journey together so let's get started.

Andrew Urban
Austin, TX

"All labor that uplifts humanity has dignity and importance and should be undertaken with painstaking excellence."

Martin Luther King Jr.

CHAPTER ONE

Sales Stage	Percent to Sales Close	Stage Description
1	10%	Why This Matters
2	20%	The Nonprofit Buyer
3	30%	Unreliable Buying Techniques
4	40%	The Other Side of the Fence
5	50%	How a Sales Process Works on You
6	60%	Sales 101
7	70%	The Nonprofit Buyer Model of Control
8	80%	Adapting to Your Organization
9	90%	Closing the Sale
10	100%	Deal done! On to the Next One...

Why this book?

Aren't there thousands of nonprofit management books out there? You bet there are. There are books and consultants to help a nonprofit organization for every conceivable topic imaginable. I'm sure you, as a nonprofit executive, are reading this humble piece of literature only by putting several other books on your list on hold. All of those other books indeed have plenty of value for the management of your organization. What value can I bring to the discussion? I choose to focus on an area I know quite well. This book is about one goal and one goal only:

<u>To help nonprofits become better buyers.</u>

What does being a better buyer mean? A better buyer is a better steward of the donor dollar. A better buyer is able to look past short-term pains. A better buyer is able to secure long-term solutions that enable an organization's growth. A better buyer is one who can create a true partnership with a vendor that works to the success of both. By presenting the strategies in this book I want to provide nonprofits the tools to secure success in what, for so many, is a painful process. I believe the process can be more effective. I believe it can be less painful for everyone. I know it can be done with a greater impact for your mission.

For the last ten plus years I have worked with and sold to nonprofit organizations of all types and sizes. My specific area has been the world that is the marketplace for nonprofit business application software which includes donor, volunteer, grant, accounting management and so forth. With that world as my background I will present much of the strategies in detail from that perspective. However, the strategies I will present as we move through this book are not exclusive to software purchases. These are easily translatable techniques and strategies to all types of purchases. I will illustrate how your most important decisions can be made apart from the sales tactics employed against you and apart from the negative internal processes that work against your own mission.

I can say, with certainty, the decision-making processes utilized by the vast majority of nonprofit organizations to purchase software to manage and grow their missions are all too familiar ineffective exercises. In too many cases I see, it is the process itself employed for a purchase that assures the organization will have trouble finding the right solution for its needs. Issues with process are not ones that only occur in the smaller, resource-constrained nonprofits, but are universal to organizations of all sizes. The scale of the mistakes made is also equal. A bad decision made at any size nonprofit can adversely affect the nonprofit on a scale commensurate with their size. The only difference is a poor purchase at a smaller or fast-growing organization can sometimes be worse than one at a large and established organization where a potentially bad decision can more easily be absorbed into a bureaucracy.

This last decade plus has been an exciting and interesting one in the world of nonprofit-specific software applications. It has seen a great deal of growth in the number and type of vendors, a round of consolidation that saw a number of big names combine, and new services and options have popped up that never before existed. A decade or so ago we were wondering if donors would ever be comfortable donating online and what kind of communication this new tool could be used for every day. In ten years we've seen several companies that were huge tradeshow sponsors be swallowed up by the likes of Sage, Blackbaud, and other long time vendors to the nonprofit world. What we have also seen is an explosion in the sheer number of vendors attempting to service the nonprofit market, an increased interest in this market from the big companies of tech (Microsoft, Oracle, IBM, SAP, etc.), and a competition of sales tactics and marketing the likes the nonprofit world has never seen before. To put it simply, it is a far more complex world out there. Making the right decisions for your particular organization could not be more important or difficult than ever. It is critical to the success of your mission. The vendors in our little part of the world have been free to call the shots, to set the table for discussions on their terms. You, in your nonprofit, with a little bit of education as to their tactics and processes, can make better decisions for your organization. With this knowledge you will be able to take control of_ the process and not be controlled in the process. That is what I will cover in this book: the means to create your own Nonprofit Buyer Model for Control within a purchasing process.

Who am I and what do I know about your nonprofit?

I have had a unique vantage point on the competitive nonprofit applications world over the last decade plus. I joined the nonprofit sector after spending over seven years walking the halls of Fortune 500 companies selling highly technical software and services. In 2000 I joined what was a little known startup at the time called Convio. While at Convio I had the privilege of working directly with the founder, Vinay Baghat, for a good portion of that time. After Convio I founded my own small company, Your Mission. For two years I worked with small to medium-sized nonprofits and had the pleasure of partnering with eTapestry and longtime nonprofit executive Jay Love. I learned a great deal in these two experiences in a very short period of time.

Your Mission grew, I appreciated the numerous speaking engagements around the country, and, in 2003, was offered the opportunity to give my customers a larger home within the Kintera fold. Kintera was actively acquiring a number of small companies. Though their appetite would eventually get a little too big I enjoyed being at Kintera as they grew from less than a hundred on staff to over 500 people with thousands of customers. I was able to work closely with the founders, Harry and Allen Gruber, and other key sales architects of the company during the four plus years I was at Kintera and was fortunate to work with so many wonderful organizations across the country. Since Kintera I have stayed active in the nonprofit arena working with Serenic Software.

I couldn't be more thankful for the twists and turns this journey has taken me on. By the benefit of my work I've been able to meet, count as friends and work with so many wonderful people who have shaped the nonprofit marketplace. I feel very privileged to have done so. These, and so many others too numerous to mention, have provided me with a unique vantage point of experience. I have been able to see the nonprofit world and its marketplace from multiple angles and in the view of many powerful personalities. The vast majority of these experiences have been positive. Some were not so great. The sum total of it all and what I have learned I hope to pass on in a constructive way that will enable you as a nonprofit executive, board member, volunteer to understand the world from the view of the vendor and use that knowledge to create effective buying processes that will serve your staff and your mission extremely well.

On the personal side, I have been in and around nonprofit organizations my entire life. I am the son of husband/wife clergy team. I joke with people that I didn't know what the word volunteer really meant growing up because whenever it said "volunteers needed" I had to be there. I guess I was "volunteered" a lot! Looking back I am glad that I was "volunteered" as I have realized how fundamental those experiences were to my thinking now. On the tech front I was that kid who was programming the church Radio Shack TRS-80 computer when something mysterious would happen to it. Before the computer was around I guess I was a direct mail expert as well...so to speak. My brother and I would help run the mimeograph drum at my Dad's church and then manually zip-code-sort the church newsletters for mailing. Who knew that experience would come in handy later on when I would be working with organizations managing hundreds of thousands of direct mail pieces and responses with giant scanners and sorters?

My personal tech background and interest took me to Dell Computer after college and from there to other sales and business development positions where I sold to the likes of Hertz, State Farm Insurance, Fortune 500 insurance companies, state/local/federal governments, etc. These were all well and good, but like many who come to work in the nonprofit world, I yearned for the passion of being able to help in the community as I had always done growing up. Not that I hadn't stayed active. Various organizations, church-related activities, children's school boards, and so forth saw my wife and I both be volunteers, event coordinators, board members, and whatever else needed doing. The thought of being able to utilize my tech background to be able to help nonprofit organizations was, and still is, highly appealing to me. The organizations that I have been able to work with, large (Heifer Project International, Boy Scouts of America, Nature Conservancy, MD Anderson Cancer Center to name a few) and small (River City Youth Foundation, local Big Brothers Big Sisters, Marywood, Hospice Austin, as well as many more) have all had a powerful impact on my life beyond the sales/vendor relationship.

And that is enough about me and my background. On we go....

How do you make a right decision?

That is a difficult question to answer. There are many different variables to a decision for every organization. Through the course of this book I will lay out a means that will help your organization lessen the impact of specific variables on your decision making. A nonprofit executive with whom I remember speaking a number of years ago told me the hardest part of his job was dealing with the variables in situations in which he was not an expert. I was surprised to hear this from this executive as he was a well-established expert in his work, very respected, and, I felt, very knowledgeable within the framework of our discussions. As he stated, the demands of his job require him to be conversant in numerous disciplines outside of his comfort range, but that it is impossible for him to be an expert in many areas in which he has to make important and expensive decisions for his organization. He admitted to me that technology decisions were one such arena. He felt that was common among his colleagues. Out of all of the decisions he has to make over time, these decisions were the ones where he felt the most reliant on others to get it right for the organization.

I let my friend know he should cut himself a break. Technology is ever-changing and can be difficult at times for anyone to discern the true benefits as there are so many particular technologies available for organizations. Add to that the new requirements from funders and the higher transparency expectations from donors and it all gets very complex. Fortunately, the actual technology components of a business software purchase are only minor aspects of the decision-making process and actually the easiest parts to control.

So how do you sort out the truth to be able to do the right thing? I let my friend know there are benefits and deficiencies in all computer hardware, software, and other services offered to his organization. To know what are the right technologies for his organization is to begin to peer through the looking glass a bit and see the other side. I began laying out to him many of the concepts I have used throughout my career to help the organizations that I have worked with find the path to their best decision. From that conversation on our relationship as vendor and organization changed markedly and for the better.

Those concepts I laid out for him are what are now in the following chapters. I have written this for you from my perspective as someone who has years of experience on the other side of the fence. I will be making that view for you through the looking glass crystal clear. With this knowledge in hand you will be able to feel confident in the decisions you make for your organization. You will be able to understand and eliminate many of the variables that are the root cause of ineffective decision-making processes. You will find the path to what can be a balanced and mature relationship with your vendors.

The first step to sorting out the truth is to understand the sales processes being employed upon you and your organization by the companies serving the nonprofit sector. Please don't take this the wrong way. I do not want you to think vendors out there are actively and intentionally trying to take advantage of you, purposefully overselling benefits, or scaring you regarding the pitfalls of not keeping up with the herd. I don't believe that to be the case on any kind of large scale. Of course, there are always bad apples out there, but thankfully those are few and far between. This book is not about creating an "Us versus Them" battle-to-death scenario in order to "win a deal." Rather, it is a model for understanding that will make your team better at the buying process and force your vendors to be better at presenting their software to match the needs and mission of your organization.

Anatomy of a bad decision

If the point of this book is to understand how to make the right decisions it is then just as important to know what a bad decision can look like. You will also have to recognize what the consequences of those decisions could be for your organization. Consider this your fair warning. I don't want this to happen to you.

An organization I knew was in the market for a complete fundraising, accounting, and donor communications solution that would tie into their HR application, payroll solution, volunteer time-tracking system, and other such systems. This may seem large, but even if you are a small organization you still have all or most of these systems, just on a smaller scale and with even less potential integration between the systems.

As they got started on their buying process, a Request for Proposal (RFP) was pulled together. A consultant was hired. The top vendors were sent the finalized RFP. The top vendors, based on the RFP responses, were brought in for initial demos and staff interviews. The selection was narrowed down to the top three vendors. More demos were delivered. Prices were narrowed down on each proposal, a committee sat down to evaluate the pros and cons of each and a decision was then made. Sounds so reasonable, doesn't it? If only it were that cut and dry.

What happened behind the scenes? The consultant, it turned out, had prior relationships with several of the vendors and had side conversations with them before and during the process. This may not always have helped with inside information, but it did give them an understanding of what to push within their proposals that would help their case. The consultant wasn't alone in this. The various vendors each had contacts within the organization that they were trying to leverage for their case as well. Some of those folks were on the actual committee making the decision. Others were influencers to those on that committee.

Members of the decision committee even had their own preferences about who the decision should go to before the process even started. As a vendor you can, after a while, start to notice these preferences by subtle terminology used by the customer that you recognize as coming from one vendor or another. It could be noticed in the questions asked during a demo, the way questions are phrased in an RFP, in basic conversations you may have with someone, or even just a remembrance you may have that the customer hung out for an inordinate amount of time at your competitor's booth at the last conference you attended. Vendors also know what customers generally came from other nonprofits and will want to bring their familiar solutions with them to their new gig. Several vendors that could have helped this organization dropped out of the running because they noticed these behind-the-scenes subtleties and nuanced interactions and figured they didn't have a shot.

So what happened with my customer mentioned above? No, I didn't win that deal, but that isn't what made it a bad decision in my book. What made it a bad decision was the outcome that I watched happen over the next year or two. After the press release announcing the glorious new partnership between vendor and customer I found out a year later that the easy part of the solution was implemented first (not a good sign), the accounting part of the solution had been taken off the table entirely once they realized it wasn't going to work within their organization without seriously large customizations that weren't understood at the point of decision, and the last part of the solution, the communications and integrations, were all on hold as they decided what should integrate with what and how. And it didn't stop there. The internal politics of the decision alienated some, caused a few very good folks at the customer organization to decide to leave, and, worst of all, new donor programs counting on the new functionality in order to move forward were postponed or cancelled altogether.

One bad decision, done in what seemed a perfectly reasonable and rational process on the surface, brought about consequences that included project delays, fundraising programs cancelled or delayed, staff departures or at least staff disaffected, and, most importantly, mission components of the organization truly unfulfilled. Even with all of that, there were folks within the organization who still thought the overall process a success. As I mentioned before, I don't want this to happen to you. This, unfortunately, is not an uncommon occurrence in the nonprofit world, but it doesn't have to be.

The Vendor Dance

I'll say this right off. I never intended to get into a sales career. I was a good old-fashioned History major in college. Upon graduation I knew I wasn't interested in being a lawyer and had given a little bit of thought to being a teacher. I fell into my first sales job at Dell and was happy as it paid the rent and I liked technology. I'm not sure that most people in sales actually start out saying "Boy, when I grow up I want to be a salesperson!" I can tell you, there are a great number of people who get a taste of being in sales and run for the hills. The first time they get shot down on the phone, the first time they are told to "cold call" prospective clients, the fear of speaking in front of groups, the sometimes uncomfortable sales questions that have to be asked are all enough to make many run away and, shall we say, find their career in other departments. There isn't anything wrong with that. To be in sales and to be good at it takes a unique set of personal qualities. Despite what you may think, many of the best sales reps I have ever known are not the loud and outgoing type. Extraverted qualities are not a requirement for being in sales. I joke with friends and family that the two biggest traits needed to be good in a sales role are a bit of Attention Deficit Disorder, to deal with the constantly changing work environment, and some set of control issues, to want to keep track of all the aspects of your latest and greatest deals. You in sales that are reading that last statement are, most likely, getting a good chuckle right about now because you see a little of yourself in that statement. If you don't that's ok, but I do believe those two traits covers a wide swath of our profession. Since we are trying to view through "the looking glass" here I am going to walk you through the lay of the land in our part of the world in the nonprofit marketplace and what the roles are like for vendor and customer.

What we as sales rep get used to, since we do this job over and over again, client by client, and year after year, is what I call "The Vendor Dance." This is my name for the back and forth that happens during a potential sale. It is different for every transaction you may have in your life. It could be personal, like haggling at a market, or impersonal, like buying a computer online. Our arena of sales is very personal. Meetings, demonstrations, tradeshows, webinars, personal phone calls and relationships are all hallmarks of the buying process for a business critical application whether you are a nonprofit or not. The Vendor Dance is done every day. You are probably involved in it right now in ways you aren't even aware. So what is it then and how am I involved in it already, you ask?

Let's think of it as being asked to a high school prom. Does she like me? I heard she does. Sally told Jimmy that Johnny thought she might sort of like me, but doesn't want to say anything in case I didn't like her first. She likes me? Great! Would you go to the dance with me? Yes! I'll pick you up at 7 p.m. in my dad's car. Translated to a sales process...What software do you think we should buy? I don't know. Let's call a few vendors? Do you think we can afford them? Tell them we're a nonprofit. Would you like a demo of our software? Do you like what you see? Maybe they want to buy our stuff? Do you think they want to buy? What signals did they give you? Did it seem positive? What else can we do? They'll buy if we do this, this, and this. Really? We can't do that. Only do this. Their legal team what? Now the board has to look at it? You can sign a contract? Great! I'll pick you up at 7 p.m. in my rental car to celebrate.

That same back and forth communication happens over and over again. I honestly still get shocked at how many nonprofits I talk to that think they are being unique in how they are trying to buy software. We still end up in the same awkward dance together unless I, as a sales rep, can begin to guide them through what I know they will need to see and do in order to make an intelligent buying decision. Some organizations I have dealt with over the years were definitely better dance partners than others -- that's for sure. However, it is clear that this is one dance in which many in our sector do need a few more lessons. The fact that these lessons may be necessary is understandable. So much focus has been put on the needed areas of board, donor, volunteer management, etc., and for good reason. This has been a neglected arena compared to the other well-studied and detailed procedures we have in so many other areas of nonprofit management. It's time we get better at this dance together.

Back when I was selling to for-profit companies, big and small alike, there was always a far more choreographed understanding of the buying process. Over the years, companies, especially the big ones, have honed the buying process from an art to a science. Each level in a company will have specific buying procedures, dollar limitations, and budget commitments along with specific instructions on how to move outside that budget in discretionary amounts. I, as a sales rep to a particular for-profit company, will know that if I'm talking to a Director at Company X that he won't be able to sign off on, or rather make the final decision to purchase, because his management level doesn't have spending authorization to afford my product. He can find, view, recommend, and be the ultimate user, but will not be the one who gets to make the final budgetary control decision. That would be one level up his chain. So I know certain sets of my sales activities will be related to him and I will also have to make sure that I secure his recommendation to the higher ups and be able to arrange a meeting there to discuss it. The best part about all of this is that he knows that too. He knows his role in the process. He knows what he has to do in order to get the budgetary approval because he has done this time and time again. It really is a dance. He knows his part of the dance. Sometimes I lead. Sometimes I follow (there is a John Michael Montgomery song in here somewhere). We both know and understand our roles and play them out in the dance until we reach the conclusion we are all hoping for. The process of the dance itself has been shaped and choreographed, taught and managed for years.

In selling to nonprofits I have found it very rare, despite the typical processes an organization will put into place for a purchase, to find one that has these same kinds of defined limits, roles, and procedures. Even if the nonprofit is big enough to have engaged in these kinds of procedures they often do not have people in the various roles used to being buyers. They aren't seasoned professionals in the dance. I have often wished I could send nonprofit executives to some type of sales training in order to help them be better buyers. I absolutely hate ever seeing a nonprofit make a bad buying decision, whether they are buying from me or not, because the impact of that bad decision is so much greater in my opinion than anything that can ever occur at a corporation. At a nonprofit it is a hard-earned, donor dollar that is wasted. That just shouldn't happen. Period.

The well-defined set of procedures corporations have used over the years to define vendors, pull together requirements, evaluate products, and make final purchase decisions has never been translated to the benefit of the nonprofit world. As a sales rep I know each one of the specific steps in a sales process, whether the nonprofit knows they need them or not, are necessary to make a decision stick. If, in the zeal of wanting to purchase something, a nonprofit is able to skip a step or two in the process it will, undoubtedly, come back to haunt them, delay the end of the sales process or cause issues during the implementation of the product. Somewhere, somehow along the line, if specific sets of questions I know need to be asked, because I've been through this process a thousand times, aren't asked, considered, or required then there will be consequences of one type or another in the end. It happens every time. Those consequences are the pain people feel when they think about what it would be like to go through another needed buying process. It's the pain of the awkwardly done dance. It's when you step on someone's toes or you assume too much that you won't get the decision you hoped for and someone will leave the dance feeling jilted. That's not a good thing.

Alright...we know that to make a good buying decision there is a well-choreographed dance to get that done. In your nonprofit you are used to purchasing applications and other large ticket items in specific ways. Is how you are doing it today the best way? My dad used to say that the seven most deadly words were "We've never done it that way before." It's time for us to try to learn this new dance together, one done in a way you probably haven't done before. Has the awkward dance you've been in led to a decision some aren't happy about when it's over? Were you really able to tell if you got the right thing or did you just get the right thing out of the options you knew about? I'm going to help you make your next vendor dance one that feels like a dance done just right, one that feels like you are on the dance floor at your senior prom with that perfect guy or girl.

I guess the saddest part of this metaphor is the fact that I got sick the weekend of my senior prom and couldn't go. Oh well. Life moves on. Fast forward to my first day of sales training at Dell Computer in 1993 - the head trainer came in and tried to put a little scare in all of the new recruits and said, "You new sales guys had better be good at handling rejection if you think you can make sales a career here." I looked up at him and said, "It's a good thing my dating experience in high school is finally going to pay off." He said I would be just fine. Thank goodness he was right.

You as a sales target

We've talked about your dance partner and the possible dance coaches. Now let's look at your role in this dance.

Your organization gets sales calls, possibly every day. Calls from office supply vendors. Calls from legal help resources. Even calls from consultants looking to expand their portfolio. For every time you fill out a marketing card at a trade show, for every time you give out your email address at a vendor website, you will be contacted by a sales team because you are now on someone's list somewhere that has targeted you for a possible sale.

It can be a hard point for many to get their head around, that when you are talking to the various vendors out there, you are, whether you know it or not, being sold to. As a nonprofit executive you must understand how you and your staff are viewed by a sales organization. We will get into much greater detail later on about how specifically I have seen nonprofit organizations make business software decisions later, but first I'd like to give an intro to how you are targeted.

Sales representatives for business application software will specifically use multiple forms of research to narrow down target segments within the nonprofit world in order to try to find what are hopefully the right type of targets to talk to in order to have the best chance of selling their particular product. Common resources include Guidestar (www.guidestar.org) which includes IRS 990 information, annual reports, contact names, and so forth for hundreds of thousands of organizations out there. ZoomInfo (www.zoominfo.com) will highlight organizations with news about the organization and its executives. Other tools will try to show spheres of influence and visually map nonprofit executives to board members who may be on multiple boards to funding sources and consultants. The internet itself has made prospecting, the art of searching for a potential sales target, much easier. I remember what it was like selling in the "pre-internet" days and it was very difficult to find even just the name of someone to try to talk to within any company. When I first started working with nonprofit organizations we had to help organizations understand why even just having a website was a good idea. Many didn't see the need and there were surveys and polls a plenty wondering aloud if donors would ever trust donating online. I'm glad that has worked out well for so many. It is just one of the many positive and landscape-altering changes in our little part of the world over the last decade or so.

Now everything a sales rep could ask for is available on an organization's website. Let's hear it for donor/funder transparency! Note sarcasm of course. The law of unintended consequences is at work here. You put all of this great information online to help with external communications to donors, funders, and others only to have all of that information readily accessible by those that wish to target you for a sales effort. In some cases all of that information readily available may have actually saved you a call or two as sales reps auto-select you out of a mailing or calling group because of the info that you have online. More often than not though the information you post online about your organization, its size, mission, and staff is used by vendors to compile list upon list upon huge list. From there those lists go to specialized firms whose sole job may be to create massive mailings that try to get as personal as mailings can get or to companies who have row upon row of personnel who do nothing but call out on those lists and execute a particular call script to attempt to gather even more information for the sales team to utilize.

As you can see, a large effort happens once you give over even the slightest amount of personal or professional information. You become "the prospect." For each prospect that is identified as a "lead" by a sales team they will then try to use a specific set of questions to decide how "qualified" a prospect you might be for their particular software. Those questions will vary from vendor to vendor, but for every vendor there is a checklist to see 1) is the organization one that fits a profile they can work well with and 2) where does this particular prospect fit in the scheme of the organization and its potential purchasing process. The sales rep will try to find out everything they can as quickly as they can because it is easier to get information early in a sales process rather than late. People tend to be more open in the beginning, a natural human tendency in getting to know someone.

One wonderful thing about nonprofit executives, from a sales rep point of view, is that they will, on average, actually call you back. They are so much nicer and less jaded about the sales process than their for-profit counterparts. Try to do "cold-calling" into a Fortune

1000 company anymore and you can hear the phones hanging up on you from here. It's a brutal way to make a living. I've lived that life and you are lucky to have one return phone call or good conversation per every two to three hundred calls. Nonprofit executives, at least in general, are a little nicer when they tell you no thank you!

A sales rep will look at your organization with an eye toward the opportunity to see if there is a right fit for their product. In the chaos of life every day in an organization there are opportunities to be the one to solve a problem, to cure a pain. To get the ear of a person who feels the acute pain you hope to solve...well...as a sales rep you have just accomplished job one, two, and possibly three in your sales process.

Conclusions and beginnings

I am going to spend a good deal of time in this book on the technical aspect of a buying process. I will try hard to make what I discuss not seem adversarial in nature in the relationship between nonprofit and vendor. No matter how much we work on putting in proper processes, on either side of the vendor or nonprofit houses, it is important to remember we are all human. Because of that we have to remember even the greatest of leaders out in our field are just like you and me. I believe when we take these relationships and make them more human rather than view them as faceless vendors or nonprofits then we all win.

My point is that we often forget that the person across the table is just as human as you or I. Here's an amusing example for you. I was on a sales call in a city that shall remain nameless with a senior executive from my company, who shall remain nameless, one nice autumn afternoon. He had flown in on a redeye flight to make an early morning meeting, didn't get much sleep, and sure enough the heavy Mexican food for an early lunch was not one of my best ideas for him. The next thing I know the warm car and the drive to the meeting took its general effect and I had a sleeping senior executive in the front seat of my rental car. Twenty minutes till the meeting and

I'm trying not to panic as I try to figure out how to wake this guy up as gently as possible while we sit in the parking lot of our next nonprofit to meet. I call my wife who, after getting in a good laugh at my predicament, calmly says to let him sleep as long as possible, then nudge him quickly, and get out of the way. I assured her that in the medium-sized rental car we were in that the "getting out of the way quickly" part wasn't as easy as it sounds. My mind was thinking of how to explain to the nonprofit we were meeting that we would be late because my exec is asleep in the car! To finish off this story I took my wife's advice. I waited till just a few minutes before the meeting, gave his arm a good poke and hoped for the best. He gurgled a bit, rolled to his right, started to wake up, asked where he was, and off we went to sell some software. Amazing. He was very good in the meeting by the way. No one ever knew of my panicked call and the calm advice of my wife. All ended well so it's ok. On to the next one.

Stories like that surprise friends of mine on the nonprofit side of the fence. They are used to seeing these vendor executives in their reputations as titans of industry and it sometimes hard to see them as the human beings they are. Being they are human also means they have their own quirks, foibles, and grudges. Another one I worked with, who speaks in front of crowds on a regular basis, confessed to me he still has, shall we say, severe tummy troubles before every speech. Another executive was so bound and determined to get his quick hotel room workout in after a long day at a tradeshow before we all went to dinner that he started doing his sit-ups in his underwear in front of our entire group of six people who were waiting to leave.

I can tell you with certainty there are some CEOs at these companies who generally don't like their counterpart CEOs very much. In seeing some of these personal rivalries I have noticed over the years it reminds me of a line from the remake of *Miracle on 34th Street* that was done in the mid-90s. The CEO of Cole's only takes on the promotion of "We'll find you what you want at the right price even if it means sending you somewhere else" because, as he puts it,

"It'll drive Victor Lambert [CEO of his main rival] nuts!" (Said while pounding his fist on the table) The executives of the companies that serve the nonprofit world are quite human. Maybe they don't have the movie-style hatred of each other as in that example, but being an executive at a company they have either founded or now lead means they also have heavy creative and competitive streaks to them.

Chapter summary

I asked at the beginning of this chapter "Why write this book?" I don't intend to tell a nonprofit how to run its business, how to serve their constituency, or organize its staff. I choose to write this book to help a nonprofit have an equal platform with the vendors out there. It is important that nonprofits are better stewards of their donor dollars in their buying decisions and be able to get exactly what they really need. It is equally important to vendors who will find their Vendor Dance partners a little easier to work with.

I believe helping to educate nonprofits in how to better manage a purchasing process will enable them to be better stewards of the donor dollar, be more apt to purchase what truly aids the organization, and have a mature, balanced relationship with vendors. My hope is that this text builds a positive construct in which nonprofit and vendor can communicate more effectively and efficiently.

In this chapter I discussed:

- ☑ The anatomy of a bad decision despite the best of intentions to do things the right way
- ☑ The Vendor Dance that has us all playing our part in the intricate buyer/seller dance whether we realize it or not
- ☑ How you are a sales target in so many ways and in so many things you do as a nonprofit professional

Having lived in both the for-profit and nonprofit world in sales roles it is clear to me that the means of purchasing at for-profit companies includes a far more mature set of processes than what we employ here in our world. There are ways in which nonprofits absolutely should not be "more like a business," but some emulation to mature our processes together in this arena is something that has been largely ignored.

Understandably, we have focused on the core topics of discussion out there (and rightfully so) such as donor prospect management, web 2.0 tools, board recruitment and management, volunteer support, and so forth, that this topic is one that plainly has not received the attention it so desperately deserves. Poor, inaccurate decisions cost donor dollars.

As we move on through this book please know the value of the donor dollar is at the forefront of my thinking. If I can help us all to do justice to the honor of that contract between a donor and the dollar spent then I will feel that this writing process has been worth every bit of my time and more. Now on to what are standard characteristics of a nonprofit buyer. If I describe you in the next chapter and you're not terribly excited about it then I apologize. It'll be ok. I promise.

Bringing it home:

- ☑ What big decisions for particular purchases were made at your organization were you happy or unhappy with over time and why?

- ☑ Think of times recently that you (perhaps also discuss with your staff) have had sales contacts with vendors. What stood out positively or negatively from those contacts?

"You are not here merely to make a living. You are here in order to enable the world to live more amply, with greater vision, with a finer spirit of hope and achievement. You are here to enrich the world, and you impoverish yourself if you forget the errand."

President Woodrow Wilson

CHAPTER TWO

Sales Stage	Percent to Sales Close	Stage Description
1	10%	Why This Matters
2	20%	The Nonprofit Buyer
3	30%	Unreliable Buying Techniques
4	40%	The Other Side of the Fence
5	50%	How a Sales Process Works on You
6	60%	Sales 101
7	70%	The Nonprofit Buyer Model of Control
8	80%	Adapting to your organization
9	90%	Closing the sale
10	100%	Deal done! On to the next one...

We are now going to turn our attention to a bit of detail on you as a nonprofit buyer. I've always been told in order to understand others it is best to look inward for understanding first. In later chapters I will spend more time on what it is like for the sales rep at the vendors, but for now let's discuss you as the nonprofit staffer, executive, board member, volunteer or other such role playing your part as a buyer/decision maker for your organization.

Know thyself

Nonprofit executives have difficult jobs. They genuinely care about the work their organization does. They are unified in their desire to do the best they can with regard to the decisions they make for their organization. That being said, even if you work at one of the larger nonprofits in the United States you still most likely have multiple jobs above and beyond your standard job description. No matter how much you may care for your organization there are items out there absolutely next to impossible for you to be able to keep up with. There are the features, functions, and requirements you may believe you need for a particular buying process based upon your job experience, but, as my friend in the previous chapter mentioned to me, it is very hard to be intimately familiar with everything out there. At some level you have to be able to trust your staff, your consultants, and your vendors.

Unfortunately, it can be confusing. Features and product sets never seem to provide easy apples-to-apples comparisons. There could be pressures from knowledgeable board members or the allure of cool technology you saw on the last webcast you attended. I have seen vendors, who are attempting to place their products in the best light possible, use the knowledge gaps they see at a nonprofit to give their company's product an advantage in your mind however they can. You may have created incredible spreadsheets of requirements, but the responses you receive back may be obscured by marketing-speak, bizarre licensing arrangements, and salesperson hype. Your "requirements" will be answered and demoed to you by the vendor from their particular point of view that shows their product in the best possible light. It isn't that the vendors are necessarily willingly trying to dupe you, but rather they are working hard to make sure they make it through the haze so you, the nonprofit executive, will see the benefits they have to offer. The presentation of all of the various options to you, no matter how organized you try to be, will begin to make you feel sea sick after awhile. They say the first step in recovery is an acceptance that you have a problem. Let's do that now. "Hi, my name is {Insert Name Here} and I've made technology decisions based on a level of faith and hope that may not have worked out as I had planned." Now it's my turn. "Hi {Inserting your name here}! It's ok. We can make this better for you."

A simple way to understand you as the buying public at a nonprofit is to understand what you are not. Let's try that now. Here is a quick list of items you may need to delegate and trust others on. This list is, of course, not all inclusive for the decisions you have to make, but is focused on the area of business software applications for the sake of our sample review in this book:

- **Features and functionality** – The details of complex business software or hardware on multiple subject-matter-expert levels.

- **Change management** – Organizational change management to the level that can explain the impact of these software decisions on your nonprofit across multiple disciplines.

- **Business process** – All of the latest business process trends affecting organizations of a similar nature.

- **Software implementation** – The implementation of complex business software on the level of a dedicated team

- **Training** – The ability to organize, staff, and implement a complete training regimen on any potential new application, software architecture, or business process.

- **Information technology infrastructure** – All of the structural details necessary for your information technology environment.

There isn't any shame in not being an expert in these items. Your job, as a nonprofit professional, is to be an expert in your own unique organizational mission. The above characteristics are items that large companies employ dozens of people across dozens of particular disciplines in order to get the right mix of corporate-shared knowledge. It is that company-shared knowledge that enables them to deliver and deploy the kind of complex projects businesses require every day. Most nonprofit organizations do not, save for a very few, have the resources to hire the number of experts that would allow them to meet the goals of a complex business software integration project. Even large organizations will typically bring in specific experts to fill gaps in their knowledge base. On top of that, if a regular-sized nonprofit did hire all of these people on staff at market rates there would not be much left for the mission!

As a buyer for any project of any real size at a nonprofit you will need to have an accurate understanding of your organization's strengths and weaknesses. It is important to be realistic regarding what strengths you have in-house and what you do not. I have seen many nonprofits go through an entire painful procurement process only to purchase software only nominally different than what they currently own. They did this because they built all of their requirements based upon their own internal corporate knowledge foundation and chose based on a lack of understanding of their own weaknesses as an organization and what could make them better.

I'd like to now put a couple of categories around what, in most cases, a nonprofit executive buyer is within his world. Mind you, I'm painting with broad strokes here. Mileage may vary.

- ☑ **The True Believer** – This can be a founder or early employee at an organization. It could also be someone personally affected or helped by the organization (a cancer survivor at a cancer-related nonprofit, for example). The True Believer is someone who I, as a sales rep, try to identify with and work with carefully, because that person may not see their own negatives (pain) or think that someone outside the organization could understand the unique nature of their nonprofit.

- ☑ **The Founder** – This person has seen the nonprofit grow from nothing to everything it is today. That experience can be a help or a hindrance. They may know everything about their organization in its present state, but may not have the broad view of the future needs as the organization grows out of their original vision. As a sales rep, dealing with a Founder is all about recognizing their contributions and then gauging how they are viewed by others internally as to their ability to be a help or a hindrance with their influence as the organization moves ahead.

- ☑ **The Wanna-Be Future Consultant** – Ah, the future consultant. These are easy to spot. Love the space, slightly cynical, sometimes feel they are being held back where they are, and, for sponge learning purposes, always seem to want to be the one who cozies up to the sales rep far more than professionally required. As a sales rep I am more than willing to accept the friendship as it will involve gaining inside knowledge of the organization I am talking to about our software. I am also careful because this person most likely is not the key decision maker at the organization.

- ☑ **The Yin and Yang of the "Program First" person vs. the "We need to be more like a business" person** – The "Program First" person believes that as much as the nonprofit is told it should get its "business processes" down to be like a business, it just can't be so. I believe the specific departmental processes businesses use are absolutely necessary to make sure the service to the mission is done effectively and accountability to the donors is attained. The "Program First" person needs to know your solution will enable the mission first and the processes that come with it are designed with the mission always at the forefront of thought. The "More Like a Business" person generally feels the nonprofit is running willy-nilly in how the various departments communicate, operate, and account for their services and dollars. They have the sole desire to see the nonprofit serve the mission more efficiently. Their message just might not be that easy to receive for some who don't want to think about their nonprofit in business terms.

- ☑ **Second Career Person** – This person is the one who has been working in the for-profit world for most if not all of his/her life and is now looking for a way to give back. This can end up being a great situation or a poor one. Either the person embraces the mission and the life of a nonprofit and is able to utilize his/her unique experience for the betterment of the organization or he/she gets frustrated at the pace of change or the inability to make people do things his/her way in a generally consensus-based decision-making environment.

- ☑ **The Silo Person, aka "Not in my job description" or "How does this affect me?"** – Change can be scary for many. Rarely can this type of person really be brought "on-board" to new change. The important item here is to make sure folks are not allowed to be obstacles to what needs to happen.

So which one are you? Maybe I should add a "Regular Old Employee" type here as a catch-all for the rest of you. The truth is the Nonprofit Buyer is, as all human beings are, a complicated organism that can mold any one of these stereotypes together.

Putting numerous human beings together to make a decision that can affect so many parts of an organization everyone cares about deeply can make a decision process quite difficult. There are many items surrounding business software applications you may not be an expert in, but knowing your mission and the makeup of your staff are your areas of expertise and the best place to start.

Knowing your own strengths and weaknesses plus how those are viewed by the vendors talking to you will help you better understand yourself and your organization as a buyer.

I want to now focus on several situations that get in the way of an effective nonprofit buying process. These are:

- ☑ "But I'm a nonprofit"
- ☑ Death by consensus
- ☑ Meeting paralysis
- ☑ Emotion in the purchasing process
- ☑ Informal buying processes

"But I'm a nonprofit."

This is a famous line inside the circles of vendors selling to nonprofits. It could also be stated something like, "You know we're just a nonprofit, don't you? So we need to really watch the budget." The translation to a vendor is typically heard as, "I probably do have some money I can spend, but I have to make sure I get the best deal I can so my board and execs don't get too upset that money is being spent on something other than program even though the purchase is necessary to be able to run the program." That's a mouthful, isn't it? The statement is also an inferiority statement. It tells me from the get-go the organization doesn't believe it can get what they need because they don't believe they are going to have the budget to do things right. The organization, by this statement, has already dug itself a hole and told itself it will be ok with a solution that is mediocre at best. The vendors to nonprofits are well accustomed to being very creative in how to help organizations afford what they are selling. You just have to ask. They want the sale as much as you want to buy. Now let's see if we can solve that inferiority complex. Ok?

It is a reality the average nonprofit probably spends 20-40% less on the same project than their typical for-profit counterpoint. Sounds good, doesn't it? As it should be? Well…vendors know that to be competitive in this marketplace they cannot generally sell software or services for the type of prices those same products and services would command in the for-profit marketplace. They just can't. This fact also makes the barrier of entry for new software companies or smaller companies looking to develop nonprofit-specific software very high. The costs for a vendor to develop and build a new solution isn't any less than what it costs to develop a solution for a for-profit company, and, in some cases, is actually more due to the specific nature of what a nonprofit may need to do. However, the vendor still can't sell the software for a high enough cost to recoup their investment in a quick enough timeframe in order to survive as a viable company. It makes for a difficult situation. Because of this the nonprofit vendor world is still a market with numerous niche vendors (church databases, scouting management, social services tracking, etc.). It is also why the biggest companies in the marketplace are either a niche of a much larger company (Sage, Infor) or just not that big as compared to the billions of revenue many for-profit focused companies have in their revenue statements. Blackbaud, one of the biggest nonprofit-only companies, for example, had 2008 annual revenue of roughly $300,000,000.[1] Sounds big enough, but not that big when you think of the $15,000,000,000 Microsoft brings in worldwide every ninety days.[2]

The fact the software is less expensive does not mean you are necessarily getting a better deal than your for-profit counterparts. It means, unfortunately, vendors are probably presenting your organization a lower end product than what you probably need because they may want to avoid any price resistance with the purchase. They may also be skimping on the estimated services needed in order to deploy the project successfully. Lastly, they are probably taking a hit to their profit margin versus a sale to your for-profit counterpart. Getting a lower end product and skimping on services can substantially hurt a nonprofit in the actual performance of its day-to-day work. Not having the right tools for a job can be lethal to getting the right job done. Not having the right mix or amount of services to implement a software project will absolutely lead to aspects of the project not being fully investigated and ultimately implemented correctly. In my experience, once a project is in and considered done, it is rare that major overhauls happen for a timeframe that can easily be in the seven to eleven years range. You are forced to live with the tool as is and make the dreaded workarounds to get jobs done in the way you need them done rather than the way the system should allow you to work. The topic for another day is how this affects morale of those who work for a nonprofit and, I believe, is a hidden component that heavily contributes to the turnover many nonprofits see in their workforce.

Next time, take the "But I'm a nonprofit" statement from another angle. An angle that says, "Hey, I'm a nonprofit. I'm different, unique, and need to make sure what I am talking to you about is absolutely right for my organization because our mission is too important to not get it right." Then you can be hard on them on the budget side, but at least by then you will know you are getting the right thing. There, don't you feel better?

Death by consensus

For sales reps not used to how a nonprofit works the idea of a consensus decision-making sales model can be difficult to adjust to. I had to adjust to it as well. I've heard selling to nonprofits compared to selling to the government with more murky decision criteria and longer waits. Obviously that definition can be a stretch, but sometimes it feels very true. Consensus building amongst a staff, with all of the competing ideas and directions, can get interesting at times. I was once at a university where I had agreed to purchase lunch for the meeting attendees. I didn't realize until I got there that eighteen people were showing up for the meeting! The old adage that food brings in the crowds holds true. A consensus management style can definitely do that as well.

A sales manager of mine once said large meetings scared him because in the room of twelve you have one person who can say yes to your product and eleven others who can say no. It is hard enough to try to sell software to an organization, but it can be extra difficult when you don't know who the actual decision makers are in the organization; who may not be a decision maker, meaning be able to say yes; and who may be able to say no even though they don't have the power to say yes. Whew! Got all that?

Consensus-making skills are valuable for any manager anywhere. For nonprofit managers, however, it is a must. Whether it is because of the type of talent pool from which nonprofits draw, if the industry itself is one that favors a consensus management style, if the pressures of the nonprofit workplace force a manager to get "input" from all sides, or some combination of this or other factors, I couldn't say 100% any one way, but it is clear the nonprofit world values and works within a consensus-management, decision-making style more so than for-profit companies.

Done well, a consensus-management style can involve all of the relevant stakeholders, allow them to feel as if they are participating in the ultimate solution, not cause the decision process to bog down in endless rounds of compromise agreements, and come up with solutions all or most agree upon. Done poorly, a consensus-management style can cause even the most efficient organizations to grind to a halt with decisions mired in endless meetings, create hurt feelings from people who don't feel adequately represented, and results in an extremely long decision-making process with which no one is happy. It isn't pretty. I have seen it done extremely well and spectacularly poorly over the years. The good ones always have an executive who can gather all input, score it correctly, and make that final decision on behalf of the organization that incorporates all of the various inputs. Where I have seen it go poorly is when opposing opinions get into a competing situation, insuring no one ends up happy. The executive sows the seed of division in the decision-making process by not providing solid leadership or by acting with an authoritarian bent. It can become a tribal war of attrition that does not benefit the organization.

A consensus-management style can work as long as in the end there is someone ultimately accountable and ready to make a decision for the best of the organization and not a decision based upon the lowest common denominator arrived at by consensus. The team at your nonprofit needs your direction as well as the knowledge their opinion is valued in these big decisions. As important as it is to know the various aspects of the mission of your organization and its staff, it is a must to know how you manage staff and how you get the best out of them. Your vendors will take a lot of their cues in how to deal with your organization in the sales process from that.

Meeting paralysis

The consensus sales model, whether done well or poorly will undoubtedly require more meetings than other types of sales cycles. Meeting paralysis is hard to avoid, especially when what happens is each meeting leads you further away from feeling comfortable with an eventual decision. A typical process of meetings can look something like this. Let me know if this seems familiar:

First conference calls with team members tasked to research options

Possible initial demo or more in-depth call with the research team

Big meeting with multiple stakeholders representing all departments

Smaller meeting with exec team

Large meeting again because we're a finalist

Smaller meeting with exec and/or implementation team

Information Technology Department review

Executive board meeting

Follow-up meeting with implementation team to review scope

Full Board Meeting

Negotiation meeting

Contract written

Lawyers involved - usually two to three rounds.

Scope concerns

Legal concerns again - another conference call

"Trust your decision" conversation if the
exec sponsor is wavering

Identification of final issues

Contract re-do one more time

Final push over the line

Sign a contract!

By my count above this would be twenty-three separate meetings or conference calls. I'm not exaggerating. Some meetings are done by conference calls, others via online conference meetings that show our computer screen online for presentation purposes, some involve the time and expense of getting on a plane, hotel rooms, rental cars, and all of that fun stuff. The hourly total all involved for the meetings alone, not including prep, study, travel, and analysis time would be roughly sixty to seventy hours alone over the course of weeks or months. Add in the rest of the prep, study, travel, and analysis time along with the fact you are dealing with multiple vendors in this process and you're looking at almost a full time equivalent employee for several months of effort if you put it all together. The pain on the staff during a purchasing and implementation process can be quite real. I've seen employees quit a nonprofit rather than go through another new product implementation! Not good!

Of course the meetings, time, prep, and research are necessary to make sure the correct choice is made for the organization. Certainly it is important to know all of the ins and outs you could ever think of before you enter into the marriage that is vendor and customer. The nonprofit marketplace does not have the same purchasing infrastructure as the for-profit world that allows for much of the company research and study of options to be done for the potential customer prior to any actual engagement of a potential customer to a vendor. That industry infrastructure is partially there with trade shows, industry magazines, journals, and the like. These are only part of the equation. As the nonprofit marketplace matures the other aspects will start to organically build themselves in. Until then, to avoid meeting overload and paralysis it is up to you to manage the process rather than let the process manage you. Limit the number of people involved in certain meetings. Bring people in on specific meetings only where it matches their specific functional areas. Have a core group that manages the process and a point person for each vendor. Don't let sales demonstrations turn into long training sessions. I've seen, more than I care to think about, long demonstration sessions turn into training meetings where the business issues at hand get drowned in a sea of specific functionality requests by certain departments that speak loudly. Talk to your vendor and ask, frankly, "What is the best way to learn about your solution?" The answers may surprise you.

Do yourself a favor. Look at how you plan to approach vendors for a solution first by understanding your own decision criteria and working efficiently with your own staff in order that all know their roles and what is required of them. It will make a consensus model work and keep meeting paralysis at bay. Your vendor will thank you, too.

Emotion in the purchasing process

One sales manager of mine told me about a national organization where he went into an executive meeting for a final presentation. After the presentation they were ushered out and told to wait for a decision. When they were told to come back in they were told of the unanimous decision to move ahead with the software and my friend was amazed to see the tears in people's eyes as they told him how excited they were about the software and what a great impact it was going to have on their mission. He was taken aback because he wasn't used to such a display of emotions in a software purchase. I found it quite a display of raw emotion of what each decision means for a nonprofit. Many nonprofit executives and employees probably feel the same way, but hold back on large display of emotions because of the fear of seeming unprofessional. Emotion is part of what it means to work in the nonprofit world. Making the process as sterile as possible does not necessarily mean a better decision will be made.

Every person who becomes involved in a purchasing decision of any magnitude will invariably become emotionally invested on some level in that process. Since we are typically in a consensus decision-making mode we have many people involved in the decision. That makes for a lot of emotions running around out there! As a fact, I can plainly state emotion takes a larger role in the purchasing process with a nonprofit organization. Why, you ask? I believe it is because of the nature of the mission of the organization itself. The same caring and feeling of being a part of something bigger than yourself most likely drew the employee to work with your nonprofit in the first place, which makes them emotionally vested in the purchase of something as inanimate as a business software application. I'm not trying to discount those who work at for-profit companies and truly love their job, their company or their chosen profession. It's just different at a nonprofit.

No matter what type of buyer that person is, as we identified in the previous chapter, that person will want to make sure, and should be encouraged, to have their voice heard in the process. As people have their voices heard, things can start getting a little emotional. I've seen it be fairly common where buying decisions become internal political footballs tossed around in a power play over the importance of one department over another, one manager over another, one aspect of the mission over another. Most nonprofits will try to suppress the emotional part of the process by bringing in an outside consultant or writing a strict request for proposal so all items from every department are itemized and represented. Some will go as far as doing both.

The emotions involved can become a positive or negative force within the decision-making process. This passion for the work of your organization is something to be harnessed for the better as you work in your buying process. The pain of previous buying processes for many can make them gun-shy at wanting to do it again. It is necessary, however, and I believe each nonprofit employee should view each buying process as an extension of fulfilling your mission. In the same way your program folks are delivering direct services on the mission, meals to the homeless or children to the shelter, by being involved in the buying process of whatever new business application software the organization needs, you are aiding the growth, stability, and work of the mission just as if you were delivering on the program side of the house yourself. It may be hard to see it that way. It is that important though. If your employees are having difficulty putting their heart into the process you will need to reiterate to them how the work on this process is critical to the future mission of the organization. Your employees have such strong emotions for your organization. Help make those emotions a positive motivator for them within this process.

Informal buying processes

A great axiom to remember: Informal buying processes automatically create decision makers out of those who shouldn't be.

I had a sales manager once tell me, "There is money to be made in chaos." What he meant by this saying is when the organization doesn't have high-quality, formal procedures in a sales process it actually becomes easier to get information and utilize back channels to influence a decision outside of the advertised sales steps. There are situations within a nonprofit that a sales team could try to understand and control to their benefit in each sales cycle. Chaos in a sales cycle is but one other way to say if you're not in control then someone else can be.

Many nonprofits are, unfortunately, extremely chaotic in their key decision-making processes. This is actually quite understandable in a strange way. So many employees at a nonprofit wear multiple hats outside of their one job description. It isn't uncommon, in my experience and I'm sure yours, to see one employee have four or five distinctly different sets of responsibilities that are quite different from their stated job title. This is admirable from the standpoint that jobs have to be done and each nonprofit hires committed people who are willing to learn other jobs for the sheer fact they must be done. This is inefficient as it means that often critical jobs are being done by those with less than a complete skill set in that arena. So many medium-sized nonprofits I have worked with have maybe one or two development people who are great at managing donors and asking for the gift, but they are asked to also be event coordinators, website development administrators, web designers, or even maybe that person who has the special delivery truck driver's license. These are, of course, diverse skills.

Multiple employees wearing multiple job hats creates, no matter what org chart you may supply or exact job title you give to everyone, an organization where the order of authority is full of dotted lines. These unofficial dotted lines give authority where it should not be and makes buyers out of those who should only be recommending a solution. Someone who may not have the executive title may, and often does, carry more buying influence than you could ever possibly imagine. Sales reps could choose to expose the weaknesses in the chain of authority and use them to their advantage. In large companies these multiple jobs are proportioned off to individuals who have a specific focus in that area of expertise. In many nonprofits, even large ones, you do what needs to be done to the best as you can because the dollars towards the mission must come first. Trying to be like a standard corporation is just not always possible. You are unique because of your mission. Embracing that uniqueness in how you manage a buying process will enable you to find that control that is extremely important.

I'll repeat it again...Informal buying processes automatically create decision makers out of those who shouldn't be. Not that a more formal buying process guarantees all is going to be well, but it is a start.

Chapter summary

In this chapter I've outlined the positives and negatives regarding the nonprofit buyer. As we have gone through who you may be as a buyer within this process I hope it has started to make sense as to how each piece you represent of yourself and your organization will affect the ultimate purchase decision you make. Vendors with whom you will be dealing are soaking it all in and making their strategies based upon the type of buyer they see you as during their discussions. You can be in control of those impressions and of the process itself.

It is so important to recognize the several main actions common among nonprofits that, in and of themselves, are positives, but too many times, become negatives. Consensus-style decision making is not an inherent negative, of course, but ensuring the process doesn't bog down requires quality leadership within the process.

Working at a nonprofit is a unique and wonderful profession. The emotions involved by the people who care about the place where they work and their desire to be involved in the important decisions of the organization are positive items. It's up to you as a nonprofit manager in charge of a buying process to not allow the positives to turn into negatives.

Next we will dig through the various unreliable buying techniques currently employed by nonprofits all over. I think you might even recognize a few of them.

Bringing it home:

- ☑ What categories of nonprofit personnel do you have working in your organization?

- ☑ How would you classify the typical managerial decision-making process in your organization (hierarchical, consensus, etc.)?

- ☑ Add up the number of meetings you had with each particular vendor in your last larger buying process. How many hours of staff time went into those meetings? Are there ways this time could have been meted out more efficiently?

- ☑ Make an internal influencer chart. Try taking your org chart, overlay the multiple job roles, and then review where the informal lines of influence may be among the different employees. This will allow you to see how the informal influencers affect a formal hierarchy when it comes to your decision-making processes.

"People don't buy for logical reasons. They buy for emotional reasons."

Zig Ziglar

CHAPTER THREE

Sales Stage	Percent to Sales Close	Stage Description
1	10%	Why This Matters
2	20%	The Nonprofit Buyer
3	30%	Unreliable Buying Techniques
4	40%	The Other Side of the Fence
5	50%	How a Sales Process Works on You
6	60%	Sales 101
7	70%	The Nonprofit Buyer Model of Control
8	80%	Adapting to your organization
9	90%	Closing the sale
10	100%	Deal done! On to the next one...

When I was a kid my Dad had these huge map books that our State Farm insurance agent would give to our family every year. When we'd go on our summer vacation Dad would meticulously highlight the route we were going to take. My brother and I would love going from page to page mapping the roads from state to state as we sat in the back of the car during the long road trips. Bottom line I learned: When you want to get somewhere make sure you have a reliable and efficient map on how to get there. Unfortunately, the decision-making process used by so many of the nonprofits I have visited over the years is not an efficient map to get the right destination.

Every salesperson you will come into contact with has been given their own map for success by their company. I learned my first "Model of Control" at Dell Computer back in 1993. It was a distinct script for phone calls, designed to guide the caller into a buying decision during the call. Dell spent years and hundreds, if not thousands, of person-hours trying to perfect a call script that would lead callers into a buying decision on the phone in an effortless and, hopefully, non-threatening manner. Dell placed us, as new recruits, in training for a full month before we could talk to a customer and, after that, we were under tight supervision for another two months with managers who would randomly listen in on our calls throughout the day to see how we were doing according to the training.

As I moved on in my sales career the trainings became more intense and included graded role plays, scenario training, negotiating skills training, and so forth. Training after intense training taught the basics of what is needed to sell a product and a company to a prospect, the tracking mechanisms for categorizing a prospect within the cycle of a deal, and how to ask the tough and sometimes awkward questions that will help get your contract signed. You would be amazed at the effort that goes into teaching someone how to "make the sale." I've often wondered why there weren't any courses for people in your position on how to be a buyer since there are so many courses for people to learn how to be a seller.

It is a reality the sales team calling on you is using a defined, learned sales process in their talks with you. If you are to get the right deal for your nonprofit you had better employ one too. Before we get to what your process should look like it's important to spend some time walking through what processes our sector typically uses today in searching for a new business software application. Every sales team calling on you has studied these processes and knows them extremely well.

So what is a "buying technique"? It's simply a means to perform the search and purchase of a particular product. There are techniques I think are helpful and those I think are counter-productive. Not every technique is all bad either. It may just be poorly executed. In its most basic form a buying process is nothing more than the dual processes of a search and a purchase utilizing, generally, a combination of buying techniques. Stating that's simplistic is only slightly less obvious than saying the sun is hot. But like the sun, our search and purchase processes have numerous elements that encompass them.

I do know the search for the right vendors to review can be a frustrating part of the equation. I remember being in the office of one nonprofit during their search for software and my contact showed me the several inches thick folders of paper that had all of the information from the vendors she had gone through in order to get down to the final two from which her organization was going to choose. There are a few large vendors that do automatically come to people's minds when they think of certain categories of software, but our sector is flush with options these days. The ability to find those lesser known vendors that could possibly help your organization needs to be fixed, that's for sure. Most use a combination of internet searches, magazine/online news sources, and referrals from others they know within the nonprofit community to find vendors to talk to about their needs.

I mentioned previously the for-profit sales world has some sophisticated search support out there for companies to find the array of tools to help them that nonprofits do not have on their side. For your nonprofit this means you will have to be extra diligent in searching for your vendors. Many nonprofits do not go any further than a Google search, a nonprofit magazine/website search, or a colleague recommendation to find options for their potential purchase. These are good places to start, but not the end most certainly.

Of these options the recommendation from colleagues is one I believe can be most helpful. The nonprofit professional community is a tight-knit community and far more willing to share experiences than your typical for-profit company. The for-profit company worries that every bit of information shared could be used against them in a competitive way. Trade groups and associations are great spots to find others with experience evaluating, implementing, and using tools like what you are probably looking for today. Search them out. Ask them detailed questions. Try to get a feeling for the details which led them to choose one package over another, the key factors in their decision. Just getting a list of names from a colleague isn't enough to start looking. Make sure to ask more than the "what" or "who" questions, but get to the "why" and "how."

Referrals are great for you to learn from, but they are also the lifeblood of a sales rep. Companies work extremely hard to cultivate positive references and will utilize referrals for marketing purposes. If you do know someone in your particular niche whom you trust to give you an honest opinion then that is very valuable. Just remember every nonprofit is different in many ways and what is good for one may not be good for your organization.

The following sections of this chapter walk through several main pieces of a buying process and what I have seen that is, and is not, being done. Understanding each of these areas is so very important for you, the Nonprofit Buyer, in order to make the best buying decisions you can.

These areas include:

- ☑ **Reliance on the consultant**
- ☑ **The infamous 'Request for Proposal'**
- ☑ **Critical business issues versus features and functionality**
- ☑ **Change management can get lost in the buying process**
- ☑ **Business processes mapping**
- ☑ **Software implementation pitfalls**
- ☑ **Training your staff for success**
- ☑ **Information technology infrastructure**

Reliance on the consultant

Consultants play a valuable role in the nonprofit eco-system. Being a consultant to a nonprofit can also become a nice career for many who spent years in nonprofit work. They gain the opportunity to work with numerous organizations, gain some potential schedule flexibility, and maybe even make a little extra money. Smart vendor sales reps love to get to know consultants. These relationships, sometimes made while the consultant was a client, can help the sales rep to gain admittance and introduction to a nonprofit organization the now consultant works with. Your consultant is not generally out to be in cahoots with a vendor. The nature of these potentially undisclosed and influential relationships can just make these introductions happen without any bad intentions whatsoever. It becomes an extension of the vendor referral gathering process.

Good sales reps do keep a reference list of what consultants work with which nonprofits in their territories that they hope to sell to. This way, when they know they need to get access to Nonprofit X, they can go to Consultant Y who works with the development department, Consultant Z who deals with the finance and operations side of the house, and maybe Board Member A who has the ear of the Executive Director. People like to work with people with whom they have worked before and know they can trust. These introductions can seem very benign and ordinary.

I have a few rules, or rather gentle advice, for hiring/working with a consultant based upon my knowledge of how a sales rep will try to work with them. Here they are:

Rule #1: Visually map tangible benefits to the organization's mission in the consultant scope.

There is a perception out there that consultants are those who often provide advice, but not value. I don't believe this to be true, but I can understand the impression since a few bad apples can spoil the bunch. I remember an IBM commercial from a few years ago where the coach is on the basketball court when the "consultant" comes in, strides up to the blackboard and outlines all sorts of plays and strategies. He then suddenly leaves while the players sit around asking themselves why the "consultant" is leaving without actually getting out on the court and doing any practice with them? The coach looks up and says something to the effect of, "Oh, they don't actual do anything. That's just the consultant." It's a little harsh, of course, but they do that to make a point. The best consultants out there, in either the for-profit or nonprofit world, provide tangible value. In the business world they contribute directly to the bottom line profitability of the company while in our world they must be able to tie their activities back to the support of your nonprofit's mission.

The types of consultant firms out there for nonprofits are varied in type and size. The nonprofit consultant landscape is dotted with everything from the small shop that is an individual or small team of former nonprofit employees to huge international companies that guide multi-million dollar fundraising campaigns. Many large and reputable firms are available to nonprofits to help them augment staff, make decisions and execute strategy. There are positive and negative aspects to their involvement. As I mentioned, if they are not able to provide a tangible connection back to the support of your mission then you should rethink your need for that consultant's particular services. On the positive side, consultants bring experience and expertise a nonprofit couldn't necessarily employ internally. On the negative side, a good deal of nonprofits I have dealt with over the years would spend more on consultants than the actual solution purchase or use them as political cover in a decision-making process.

Rule #2 on hiring a consultant: Keep institutional knowledge sacred and in-house.

I personally think too many nonprofits spend too much money on consultants. I believe it becomes a budget trick where full-time staff can be deemed too expensive to hire and difficult to fire if the financial situation changes, or the extra cost of staff can look bad on the expense side of the ledger for the annual report. Consultants are easy to hire, easy to fire, and are a fixed cost. No insurance costs, unemployment insurance, and all of the other management hassles. Almost every nonprofit I have ever been around sees staff in a more personal role than most for-profit companies I've known. Staff members become family because of the shared belief in the cause. It is understandable there can be a hesitancy to hire when there could be the prospect of having to let a member of the family go at some point in the near future. Easier to bring in the consultant to do a targeted job and move on. This, unfortunately, doesn't help the organization in the long run, by leaving institutional knowledge of various programs, fundraising efforts, and more outside the organization itself. I believe consultants should be a supplement and support to the internal full-time nonprofit staff and not counted on for core functions critical to the long-term success of the mission.

Rule # 3: Disclose all past relationships and biases

Depending on the consultant you hire, you could very well be automatically ruling out a number of qualified vendors or solutions to review because of that consultant's background, past history, and business relationships. They may purport to be unbiased in their work and be perceived that way by their former clients, but a pattern of the types of clients that person works with and what vendors they end up working with for those clients is generally evident with a little digging. As an organization hiring the consultant you should consider these questions as standard fare for their "background check," so to speak. Ask the consultant what vendors they have personal relationships with, not just business affiliations - two totally different questions. Ask what vendors they personally trust, which ones they don't trust and why. If they are a former nonprofit executive, ask them what vendors they worked with when they were on your side of the house. Were they a consistent reference for anyone and why? These are just a few suggestions which could help you understand more about the person you are hiring to be your organization's consultant.

One amendment to the above: Hiring a firm versus hiring an individual consultant

If you are hiring a firm also be sure to do the best you can to know who is going to be actually performing the work. That is usually a moving target as people are on and off jobs sometimes rather quickly. Firms will tell you it is first come first served to individuals on staff and they can't hold staff off on one job while waiting on another. That is true because the company does not make any money when the consultant is not billable. Unless you are a huge client to the firm they won't keep one particular consultant on hold for you. They can't for the sake of their business. I liken it to the founder of Southwest Airlines, when asked why his planes had the fastest turnaround in the industry between flights, said something to the effect of, "We don't make any money when the planes are on the ground."[3] All you can do here is get as much information as you can. If you sign your contract and a consultant shows up who you have not been able to vet, then I would do it right then and ask similar questions as above and keep going until you are satisfied with the individual who you are going to be spending so much time with and who will be supporting the mission that you are, of course, very passionate about. Your mission itself is worth asking the extra set of tough questions.

The point of spending this time discussing consultants here is many at nonprofits do see them as something outside of the sales process or someone who only facilitates a sales process. It is my experience consultants, many times, are actively involved in the sales process as willing or unwilling counterparts. It is the nature of their relationships and communications. Again, I don't believe your consultant is a nefarious and devious plotter out to make money by recommending various vendors over another. I have just seen too many situations where the natural course of personal relationships makes their way into a business recommendation in inappropriate ways. I'll tell my kids sometimes accidents often happen when you're not paying attention (they aren't fans of that phrase!). What I am saying, with regard to consultants, is to pay attention, ask the tough questions, and then you'll be able to get to work together confidently.

The infamous "Request for Proposal."

This is what many in the nonprofit world see as the Holy Grail of the business-like buying process. The Request for Proposal (RFP) is also what so many people, inside and outside of nonprofit organizations, absolutely despise: a hundred-page document with eight separate cost worksheets all lumped together with requirements derived from interviews with all of the key "stakeholders" in the organization. It looks great to the board who is overseeing the process, to the consultant who gets to show a thick document that displays in vivid color all of the value that they brought to the table, and to the staff who look smart for trying to codify everything they need. For some places, like government and higher education, and many other entities, standard policy states the RFP as a required step in order to purchase a product. I don't predict that this buying technique, and it is just one technique commonly used within a buying process, will ever go away, nor should it. What I will illustrate is what I see as the main problems with this technique today and hopefully we can make the process better for all of us.

- ☑ **It can potentially codify only what you know and not what you need.** I find RFPs are almost never written in a way that elicits education from the responses. It documents what you know is true based upon your own experience and is not designed to extract what could be potentially available out there to make your organization better. The rote spreadsheet of 300 questions are written by staff interviews telling a consultant or staff delegate what they want to do better based upon their current job. This is well and good and captures the specific pains of the organization. However, if the documents could be written to gather responses about what is not in the current staff knowledge base, then that would be a far more useful document for your organization to use in a buying process. How do I know what is out in the future you ask? Tough question. Agreed. The best RFPs I have been able to respond to have had sections in them with regard to future direction of my company's product, examples on future growth strategies of the nonprofit organization and how our company's solution could adjust to those challenges, or a free-form section asking for tangible evidence detailing our experience and specific capabilities for helping nonprofit organizations like theirs (specific mentions were made to avoid marketing-speak and press release materials), and so forth. Another thought, based on what I have seen, is where the nonprofit organization has expanded the interviews for information gathering outside the stakeholders at their own nonprofit and gone to interview other nonprofits which they wanted to emulate.

- ☑ **Responses are easy to manipulate.** Maybe manipulate is too harsh a word here, but then again maybe not. I've seen some scary things go out in RFP responses. The responses to your RFP can get dicey in that the RFP is written by the staff members who may lack knowledge about how other application systems work. Thus, the questions in an RFP are written out of the experience and understanding the staff has about their current system, the one causing them all of the pain. If I don't answer the question in a way that illustrates what I can do for them differently than the system they are trying to replace then I'm not doing my job very well. Am I answering the question exactly as the nonprofit is requesting it be answered? Maybe not. Am I answering it in a manner that will hopefully educate them on my solution? Yes. I have seen vendors take this technique to an extreme end that pushes the answers into the manipulation arena. It's not pretty. I was involved in a sales process a number of years ago that was run by a consultant who was a current vendor to the nonprofit in question. We knew via prior dealings with that consultant the RFP would be written to try to weed us out of the process. I don't believe the organization knew the consultant was doing that. They didn't know the back channel dealings between us as vendors. When we did receive the RFP it was readily apparent the questions were written so that we would have to answer "no" over and over again. What did we do? We answered "yes" over and over again except for the biggies that were absolutely no. Where we answered yes we explained how we would do that within our system even though it wasn't in the vein of the questions. Was it the right thing to do? By doing so we were able to get ourselves out of the first round of eliminations and in front of the customer instead of just the consultant. We eventually won the business on our merits, and we and the consultant company kissed and made up. The important thing is the client went on to a successful project. This can happen in even the most stringent of RFP processes.

- ☑ **No relationship equals no response.** Many vendors won't respond to an RFP if they don't have a previous relationship with the organization. The general belief is, and it is true more often than not, an RFP is won by a company that is in there with an earlier relationship with a staff member, a board member, or consultant. When I see a firm running an RFP process for a nonprofit, one of my first questions is whether or not they are bidding on the project against the rest of us vendors, in effect wiring the project for their own company. Sort of like Dick

Cheney running George Bush's VP selection. Guess what? I'm the best choice! Tell me this...how many grants do you apply for where you don't have some sort of relationship or ability to get info on the selection process? Not many, I would bet because the odds of winning that grant are much slimmer than other choices. You go where you have a relationship or some sort of in and understanding of the decision process. You wouldn't bet your grant funding on blind faith grant proposals, so why do organizations think vendors would do the same with a blind RFP request where there is no opportunity for communication or relationship prior to having to submit a response? Real discussions are necessary, not just bidder's conferences with pre-submitted questions. It's important to have staff available to vendors prior to the formalized process for open and honest discussions. That extra time to get to know the various vendors will absolutely lead to your next RFP gaining a larger response return rate. This bullet point leads to the next point which is…

- ☑ **My writing is so much better.** Many vendors believe the best RFP is one they got to help write. You may be asking what in the world I'm talking about. It really does happen. I've had potential customers ask for sample RFP response documents of mine and the RFP that comes back to me looks awfully familiar. If you've done this long enough, as I have, you can start to see patterns and know by verbiage in the RFP what vendor the organization has either been talking to or favors already. That right there will cause a vendor to not respond to your RFP, possibly to your organization's detriment.

- ☑ **Like giving an A to a paper based on weight.** The bigger the document obviously doesn't mean the better it is, but some people just love to send out huge documents. I've toiled hours upon hours having to answer circular questions in separate sections of an RFP where it becomes obvious one side of the house was not talking to the other when they put the document together. The same questions are asked over and over again in different ways on different pages. That seventy-five-page RFP that comes to me becomes my 150-page response with nine appendices. It really does get silly sometimes. I've personally sold multi-million dollar deals in the for-profit world on two pages of requirements and a three-page proposal response. If everything you really need to know about a vendor and a product can't be summed up in a succinct document, then you are asking for confusion by obfuscation.

☑ **CYA.** The massive RFP is too many times a CYA document. Hopefully you know what that acronym means and I don't have to be crude. It means the leadership of the nonprofit may not want to stand up to its staff, its board, or its constituents and make a decision and will use the process of the RFP document to cover their... Maybe they are bullied by a micro-managing board or nagged by a staff who all may be fighting about their own idiosyncrasies of their day-to-day jobs, or are paralyzed by the need for the ultimate consensus. Who knows what the reason is. There are many. All I do ask is, before you start an RFP process, make sure you are doing it for the best of reasons.

Lastly, RFPs can be a great source of information and a logical way to sort out one vendor over another, if done well. If you do want to get the broadest set of responses, the best efforts in those responses, and the most creative solutions to your issues, then the RFP needs be but one technique within your overall buying process and not the sum total of the process. Take the good things, discard the bad, add in the best new ideas, and you will learn a great deal more from your vendors the next time you send out an RFP.

Critical business issues versus features and functionality

Our next typical problem is beginning the process by letting people define the features and functionality they want out of their new system rather than first defining and gaining consensus on what are the critical business issues before the organization.

What is a critical business issue? It is an issue to be solved that, without which, an organization cannot operate or remain viable in a particular business process. If a critical business function is interrupted, an organization could suffer serious financial, legal, or other damages to its mission.

Later on we will discuss a process for defining your nonprofit's critical business issues (commonly called CBIs). What happens too often is the staff is laser-like focused on what they do on a day-to-day basis and, when asked to come up with ideas of what they would like out of a new system, start to talk in terms of fixing function A that causes daily pain in process B. These low level details are important, but may not be important to all or even a driving reason of the value of a new system. This type of thinking is how we end up with the RFPs that have massive spreadsheets of individual feature-sets, but very little opportunity for the vendor to talk about how they can provide a total solution for the organization's environment.

My point is every organization first needs to understand the overall pains they are hoping to solve before starting a buying process, the high level bucket lists they can easily rally around, explain to a board, and communicate to vendors. From there, the specifics of feature/functionality will begin to tail out from those pains in a specific order or importance based upon the features' proximity to helping solve a part of the overall pain. These are far more important to understand before embarking on the feature and functionality journey which defines most nonprofits pre-sales cycle purchase process.

Change management can get lost in the buying process

Business, no matter how you slice it for either a nonprofit or for-profit business, is about constant change. Change management is the ability to understand how the purchase you are embarking upon is going to alter the as-is business processes of your organization and how best to optimize them for the new system. Every new system being deployed is disruptive. It's disruptive to your pocketbook, to your staff who may be used to doing things one way or the other, and, almost always, to how different departments communicate and interact. Organizations become so intent on the purchase, installation, and training on their exciting new system that how to internalize the changes the system is bringing to them are often given short shrift. The vendors can be guilty of this as well as they are so worried about coming in on a high cost that these services are among the first on the chopping block when it comes time for a cost proposal.

The hope is staff interaction during the implementation process and heavy training will take care of it enough. Without this type of work though it would be like putting regular gasoline in a Formula One race car. It may run, but you probably won't get the best performance. Change management provides the roadmap for organizational success with the new product. Take the time to model your own business processes and mark where the inefficiencies are in your work. Knowing where you have been and are now is just as important as knowing where you want to go. Instilling proper change management will make sure where you go doesn't feel like where you have already been. This is an important piece of the puzzle that by so doing will make sure you are asking your vendors for the right solution for your organization.

So many organizations I have worked with over the years do not take the time to smell the roses. They are so intent on the day-to-day work that the processes needed to run their business become incredibly informal, relying on relationships to make them work. If certain people leave the organization then that process suffers. It is important you not only know your staff, but also know how your staff works. To do that you must make sure that your business processes are codified somehow and accessible somewhere.

I remember working with Big Brothers Big Sisters (BBBS) and they could tell me exactly how much it cost them to place a Little with a Big. They knew and had mapped the entire process for vetting a potential Big down to the granular level and knew how much staff time it took to review the forms, make the interviews, background checks, and so forth in order to qualify the person to be a Big. This information was amazingly helpful for them as they had readily available for potential grant funders how much the business processes of their mission cost them. They could easily tell a grantor how many Bigs a $10,000 grant, for example, could fund. As they always had a waiting list of Littles, BBBS had a great story to tell potential grantors how their dollars could go directly towards the mission. They knew this because of a process most nonprofits do not take the time to do: business process mapping.

Business process mapping is the term that refers to the activities involved in defining exactly what business functions your organization does, who is responsible, to what standard a process should be completed and how the success of that business process can be determined. Once this is done, there can be no uncertainty as to the requirements of every internal business process. Every best practices business book out there requires a business entity to follow a process approach when managing its business and to create visual maps of their processes. The business then works towards ensuring its processes are effective, efficient and continually improved.

Many books and techniques for process mapping exist. I'm not going to suggest one over the other or say you should put massive resources towards doing this for every part of your organization. What is important though is to understand the business of your own mission.

Whatever means you use to map it you will find some things will make you scratch your head and ask why. It is always a good exercise to do even on a minimal level, to give root to the pains that are your Critical Business Issues (CBIs) in a purchasing process. If your organization doesn't have a formal business mapping exercise then you most likely do it in an informal manner fairly often.

It would be hard to run your nonprofit if you didn't understand how certain processes get from A, through B, and over to endpoint C. With a little formalization of this process you can find your way to defining your CBIs in a more concise fashion.

The four typical steps of process mapping[4]

- ☑ **Process identification** – attaining a full understanding of all the steps of a process.

- ☑ **Information gathering** – identifying objectives, risks, and key controls in a process.

- ☑ **Interviewing and mapping** – understanding the point of view of individuals in the process and designing actual maps.

- ☑ **Analysis** – utilizing tools and approaches to make the process run more effectively and efficiently.

Software implementation pitfalls

Isn't it just like loading some software on my computer? Not really. There is always a bit more to it than that. Sophisticated business application software will require a set of implementation tasks to be done that matches the environment in which they are being placed. Accessory applications, database infrastructure, integrations to other applications, and even things that seem minor, like operating system service pack upgrades done at the right timing during an implementation, are vitally important to be done right the first time or risk steps further down the line in your setup. Implementation services numbers can get very tricky to understand for many potential users. I have seen vendors use these numbers in a variety of ways. The nefarious way is to lowball a bid with an expectation of making it up on work later thus forcing your competitors into explain mode. In your shoes, I would feel like this bid is the bad plumber who comes and says your job will be done in a day and next thing you know they are drilling holes in your foundation and having their mail delivered to your house. Taking in bids on a retainer basis can make you feel like you are signing an open-ended agreement on faith hoping it will work out how the vendor says it will. Fixed bids may seem nice, but the vendor will have to build in extra profit in their bid to cover their risk. I've seen organizations try to quantify service dollars into specific task or functionality lines, but that only works to a point because even the most honest vendor will try to place their numbers into that scenario in the best light they can.

There aren't too many reliable ways for a nonprofit to be absolutely positive the application they want to implement will be done for the exact dollars. The best that can be done is to be dealing with a reliable vendor, checking your references, and other such activities. Most projects I have seen over the years do not necessarily die a painful death solely because of a vendor. As is the case in most divorces, there is generally enough blame to go around. It's still painful, of course. Nobody wants to see a project go south. The vendor doesn't want to see it because the bad publicity will hurt future sales and trying to fix it will cost significant sums of potentially unbillable hours. You in your nonprofit don't want to see it go badly because you probably don't have the time or resources (dollars, staff, or otherwise) to start over. Make sure you have a dedicated resource plan for your implementation that has committed staff from the vendor and yourself. Working together and keeping expectations aligned are the best way to avoid issues and cost overruns in an implementation and will overcome just about any hiccup that may come along.

Training your staff for success

Training is one more of those items that gets missed. In the rush to go live on your new software, training can get a little lost and become a sorely missed afterthought. Users who don't want to be away from their jobs for a day or more at a time to learn something new and frightening, along with mismatched training methods for the type of users involved, can make the transition to a new system begin with a thud for many. It doesn't have to happen. Too many nonprofits I have worked with, in their rush to get to the features and functionalities in their requirements, forget the line item for training and don't properly have their vendor outline how their training will be delivered.

It's important to plan an end-user training strategy before you begin to roll out new software. Set your training goals by dept. or job function, assess your users and their individual training needs, and ask your vendor what type of training delivery methods they offer. A training program outline offered during a proposal process seems like a no-brainer to have, but for so many it just is not there or is glossed over.

Information technology infrastructure

This one is listed last on purpose and is truly short and sweet. Business needs must define the infrastructure needs and not the other way around.

Defining your features, functions, and requirements you believe you need out of the software you are looking for is far more important than whether or not you want an in-house or hosted solution, a Microsoft-based or Linux open source solution, what database back-end needs you may have, the hosted portal requirements, and many, many other ins and outs to worry about. Too many nonprofits allow their IT staffing capabilities to dictate what particular type of solution they can look at. Thus, they are allowing the technical concerns to overrule the business needs. That is not a recipe for success. In sales we typically talk of the "technical win" meaning we have agreement with the client that our solution is technically feasible for the client and can fit into their office environment and the "business win" which means we have won the day with the critical business issues identified. The problem with too many organizations in the buying process is the "technical win" outweighs the "business win" and that is a recipe for failure.

Chapter summary:

Like the maps from my childhood roadmaps, having a plan on how to get to your destination is critically important. Knowing where you are starting from (Business Process Mapping, Change Management review, technical infrastructure review, CBIs), how you're going to get there (Consultant support, RFP process, vendor reviews, etc.), and where you want go (CBIs, process openness and communication, and information gathering) when combined will get your organization a vast set of improved vendor responses and support in your next buying process. More information from more sources arranged in a logical, concise manner detailed by your team will help alleviate some of the pain from buying processes of the past. Now we will move on to the view of nonprofit organizations from the other side of the fence.

Bringing it home:

- ☑ Do you rely on a consultant or consulting firm? If so, have you had the conversations with each surrounding the rules listed in this chapter?

- ☑ Review your last RFP process. What worked, what didn't? Did you receive the number of responses you thought you would? Were there vendors you thought would respond that didn't? Why do you think that was?

- ☑ In your last or current buying process are you able to articulate three to five main critical business issues for the project that must be solved in order to deem the project a success?

- ☑ What does your organization have in the way of business process mapping for the mission?

"The purpose of a business is to create a customer."
Peter Drucker[5]

CHAPTER FOUR

Sales Stage	Percent to Sales Close	Stage Description
1	10%	Why This Matters
2	20%	The Nonprofit Buyer
3	30%	Unreliable Buying Techniques
4	40%	The Other Side of the Fence
5	50%	How a Sales Process Works on You
6	60%	Sales 101
7	70%	The Nonprofit Buyer Model of Control
8	80%	Adapting to your organization
9	90%	Closing the sale
10	100%	Deal done! On to the next one...

The Peter Drucker quotation at the beginning of this chapter illustrates the conundrum vendors who sell into the nonprofit sector face every day. What is it like being a for-profit company trying to sell to a nonprofit organization? Is that an oxymoron? Yes? No? Is it any different than selling to small businesses, large businesses, or governmental agencies? What is it like on the other side of the fence? Is the grass greener? Maybe. Maybe not. Let's see if we can answer these questions...

As a sales rep I have to understand and be able to work with the peculiarities and nuances that come with the nonprofit space. I have known quite a number of sales reps who have tried to work with nonprofit organizations and could not deal with the idiosyncrasies and differences that come with the territory. The motivations nonprofits have as compared to your typical businesses and how to deal with the decision cycles different from most businesses are the types of things that throw some aspiring nonprofit salespeople into fits. It is a different world out there than what many professional sales reps are used to or can professionally manage. The reps who can't manage dealing with these differences can come off like a bull in a china shop to their nonprofit customers. They typically do not last long in our part of the world.

The same can be said for companies who dabble in selling to nonprofit organizations, but soon move on because they have a hard time understanding how to manage the differences inherent in selling to nonprofits. I can't tell you how many local system integrators or consultancy shops I have seen over the years which try to make an extra little bit of business selling their services to a nonprofit and end up realizing they can't make it the main part of their business portfolio. They may even have a philanthropic commitment in the community and want to help here and there, but they ultimately will say they need to sell to businesses because they "can't seem to make money selling to nonprofits." Money can be made selling to nonprofits. It just requires a different mindset, a different kind of commitment.

Lastly, it requires a different type of sales team. Those sales teams generally fall into a few general categories. Let's get to know them shall we?

Know thy vendor

Being good at the Vendor Dance means knowing your partner in the dance well. The best dance partners make dancing with them feel effortless and smooth. In our nonprofit world there are a whole different set of vendors than the regular old for-profit world where I started my career. It has started to blend a bit more in the last few years as many traditionally for-profit servicing companies have made forays into the nonprofit sector. When I began my career with nonprofits I had to learn what the various types of vendors were and how they related their specific functionality to the needs of the nonprofits I was talking with every day. By learning them I don't mean just learning what categories they would fit in based upon the type of functionality they offered, but rather, in what type of primary means did they attempt to establish a relationship with you, the sales prospect.

As it is in war you should know your enemy prior to engagement. Of course salespeople are not your enemy, but you must have the recognition that a vendor is employing a carefully designed and crafted tactical strategy on you. There is a formula and study to these strategies and tactics that I will detail in further chapters. I will explain the reasoning behind each step and how they are meant to bring you to a favorable decision. These tactics are designed to place their products in the best possible light in order for you to come to the positive end result of a purchase of their product. This is all fair as in love, war, and advertising of course. As we all know, 4 out of 5 dentists agree Ford trucks are built Ford tough. Messages and images are carefully crafted and focus-group tested in our world today. Welcome to Capitalism 101. It is alive and well...even in the nonprofit sector.

All of these companies selling their wares to you need to make a profit of course. Making a profit is a positive thing if you are a customer of theirs and you should hope they do make a profit. Those profits are how they are able to reinvest resources back into the product you purchased and hopefully make it better and better over time. The fact they are out to make a profit and are employing a strategy does not, of course, make them a rapacious capitalist out to rob your organization of every last dollar and leave you with an awful product. The positive takeaway here is, in my experience, with so many varied vendors serving the nonprofit world the vast majority of them are very much like you. They care about the nonprofit community and are trying to find their own unique way to serve and be involved. Most believe in their products and want to do their best to make you successful with them.

What I would like to do is describe four broad categories of vendors for you. If you have dealt with a sales team selling to your organization in the past this will seem familiar to you from a gut feeling, but most likely you haven't been able to put your finger on exactly what you were dealing with. As you read on I hope these categories don't sound too awfully cynical. Please do not mistake any of the overall critique below as an indictment on everyone who occupies each of these categories. I assure you most of the vendor representatives you do deal with have positive motives in their life as to why they have chosen to try to work with nonprofits via their company.

Here are the categories:

- ☑ **The "I'm one of you"**
- ☑ **The Predator**
- ☑ **The "Doesn't have a clue about nonprofits"**
- ☑ **The Lifer**

The **"I'm one of you"** vendor is one who can empathize with you as they have, as you, lived in it for years. They may have even come to the company from an NPO background. I liken this approach to the "I liked it so much I bought the company" sales pitch from the old electric razor days. These folks bring a great deal of credibility with them and a wealth of war stories of days gone by that will impress you. You probably felt like you were at a NPO luncheon talking with a colleague more than you have someone there selling a product to you. They may have even have been a colleague in the past. Do not be mistaken. They do have a job to do and are there to sell you something.

I remember a debate early on with the Kintera sales team, centered on whether Kintera should hire salespeople who understand nonprofits or nonprofit people who could sell. The problem was that so few professionally-trained technical salespeople that were used to selling to corporations were able to get in and understand what drove a nonprofit and how to connect to the people making the buying decisions. They were used to a different pace and style in the buying process. The nonprofit professionals coming into a purely numbers-based sales organization had a hard time dealing with the pressure of the sale and weren't usually comfortable asking the tough, but required, sales questions of those who may have been their colleagues just a few months prior. So whereas the person across the table may be "one of you" over the life of their career it is important to remember their goals, their pay structure, and career advancement do not necessarily line up with the success of your project or long term needs of your mission. If they are good at their job then they will use their experience to find the means that match your needs, which they will understand oh so well as they have walked in your shoes, with the benefits of the product they are representing.

I'm not asking you to be a full blown skeptic, but rather a healthy one. No vendor is truly one of you because there will always be that barrier there of for-profit company goals as opposed to the nonprofit mission success. Your goal with the "I'm one of you" salesperson is to make sure they show that their application goals align themselves with your mission as closely and succinctly as possible.

The Predator is the person or company who usually doesn't have the wealth of NPO background or can't engage you with war stories like the first vendor type described above, but knows software or other technology aspects extremely well. This person is convinced your organization would be better if only they followed the business principles they learned from X number of years at Big Company Y. They prey on your perceived lack of "business" experience and see your nonprofit organization as the next mountain to be conquered into submission. You may be impressed by their knowledge and their confidence and assume they must know what they are talking about since they have all of this corporate experience and are now just trying to "give back." They seem like it is their mission in life to show you how things should be done. Don't be mistaken. They are also there to sell you something.

The predator, the negative connotation of the word notwithstanding, can come in what is a very friendly form. Many times it can be in the form of a generous board member or community member who cares about your cause and would like to help by donating at least a portion of their services or software. You know who these people are and you need and want their help, but feel the sting as they believe they know how to run your organization better than you do even though their total monthly time commitment is roughly four hours per month. Even if their consultants are being offered pro bono or the software tools are being offered at a significant discount compared to their "regular" customers remember the hidden strings that can come with pro bono at times. I have heard the phrase "the high cost of free" many times. How true is that statement? Amazingly true.

The "Doesn't have a clue about nonprofits" is one my favorites. This person is typically someone the nonprofit-specific vendor hires out of the technology world (a former high tech representative for example who may have worked at one of the biggies like Dell, Microsoft, Sun, Oracle, etc. for example). This person is trained to the hilt on how to sell complex technology solutions to Fortune 500 companies. This person knows the ins and outs of all of the sales philosophies and can talk a great game about how to sell by a process. The only problem is nonprofits are just plain different. They don't understand how to talk nonprofits language, what's important to a nonprofit, or how decisions are made within a nonprofit. This is my favorite group because usually about six months to the day into the job they will come to me and say something to the effect of, "I just don't understand why I'm not gaining any traction here. Nonprofits just don't know what they are doing enough to understand what I'm trying to sell to them." I'm always amazed at when these reps blame the nonprofits for their lack of understanding rather than realizing their job in sales is to first understand their potential customers and not the other way around. Not surprisingly, this type of vendor rep doesn't usually have a long career in our wonderful part of the world.

The Lifer is the most positive of the categories. I credit the name of this category to David Lawson, the pioneer of donor analytics for nonprofit organizations. It is how he describes himself and his desire to serve the nonprofit sector in his life's work. I believe this category encompasses the best pieces of the above categories and includes most of the people at the vendors you deal with on a regular basis.

This is the category I try to keep myself in every working day I am talking with an organization. My personal story includes a great deal of the same desires to help, to give back in some way, to find meaning in my daily work as those at the organizations I work with every day. Those reasons are why I and other "Lifers" like me choose to work in this amazing sector. The hardest part of being a "Lifer" is balancing the work realities of a sales quota and the business pressures with what I know are the practical realities of and the caring I have for the nonprofit world.

Knowing your dance partner, as you can see, is quite important. I encourage you to have the discussion with your salesperson and ask them to describe themselves, how they came to work in the nonprofit world, and understand what charities they are or have been involved with in their daily life. By doing so you can gain an understanding of what type of dance partner you are working within your buying process.

The Consultant

To follow-on from the previous chapter I'd like to talk about consultants from a different angle now, as a vendor. The nonprofit world, like the business world, keeps the eco-system of consultants alive and well. Major corporations spend billions (Billion with a B!) of dollars with large consulting companies to insure their business processes are aligned across multiple business units and across multiple countries. For the companies they serve they provide services for corporate technology projects, finance support, auditing services, and even complete outsourcing of whole divisions and departments.

In the nonprofit world the typical consultant doesn't necessarily outsource an entire department, but they will outsource particular functions or augment a department. Development departments will hire a consultant to run an event or plan a capital campaign. An IT department at a nonprofit will hire a consultant to help manage a "Request for Proposal" process to purchase new systems. The list of the kinds of projects and types of consultants a nonprofit will hire are as varied as those in use by major corporations.

Working with a consultant can be a great shortcut to getting that intelligence. Once the sales rep knows which consulting firm or individual works with your organization they will attempt to work with those folks in order to gain a higher level introduction to the organization than they ever could on their own as well as gather a firsthand understanding as to whether or not there is a real need for their product. Sales reps will hope some of the credibility the consultant has with the organization will rub off on them. These relationships are critical to a sales rep if they want to gain quick access to the decision-makers in an organization. The consultant can be, for the vendor sales rep, an important piece of internal human intel to understand the personality of the organization and what path the sales rep needs to use to facilitate a decision.

Realizing the consultants who work with you are part of our Vendor Dance in ways that may not have been seen to you is important to know. Some consultants are on your side, some will be on your vendor partner's side, while the best ones are coaches who bring the dancers together and enhance their chemistry.

What a sales team must understand about nonprofits, but sometimes forget

The sales team that sells to a nonprofit must be able to understand and work within how the nonprofit world runs. To do that, one must study the sector and, hopefully, become a part of it. I had a fellow rep tell me once he found selling to nonprofits to be like selling to the government without the budget and processes. That isn't necessarily a flattering analogy, but it does fit sometimes.

What that rep didn't understand was how to match the sales needs of his company with the realities of the decision making nonprofits live under every day, which we will now explore. A sales team who has worked with nonprofits for any length of time will see the following categories as normal. The point of listing these out like this is not to detail the difficulties of selling to nonprofits, nor to state these difficulties are more challenging than any other type of sales.

If you, in managing your buying process, can change up or clarify these norms with your vendors, then you will shortcut several unnecessary steps in the Vendor Dance and get straight to the information you were looking for all along.

These general norms are:

- ☑ **Sales cycles can be longer at a nonprofit than in the for-profit world.**
- ☑ **Nonprofits are budget-sensitive on all levels.**
- ☑ **There are so many new ways to lose a deal when working with nonprofits.**
- ☑ **Formalize within the informality of the typical buying process.**
- ☑ **Understand the mission focus.**

Sales cycles can be longer at a nonprofit than in the for-profit world.

Let's start with the extremes: the for-profit company and the government of all levels (federal, state, local).

In the for-profit world there is an incentive to be able to make a decision and move forward with a project. The profit motive and desire to get ahead of your competition make for strong forces to help get a company to sign on the dotted line and do the deal. Sales teams that focus on your standard for-profit companies tie into growth needs, efficiency concerns affecting the bottom line, and other such motives in order to sell their products. Selling to a for-profit business can have a long sales cycles here and there, but the key is you have extremely powerful incentives to close the deal, no matter if the company is doing well or poorly in its given market segment.

The government, on any level, buys a lot of stuff. Selling to the government can require filling out lots of forms and complying with tons of regulations about how you do business. Huge companies that sell to the federal government, for example, will base their entire sales effort for a year on the annual federal procurement list. In these sales you may have a long sales cycle and a boatload of rules to live by, but the budget is certain and the fact a decision will actually be made is generally a given.

In learning to sell to a nonprofit the typical for-profit sales rep needs to understand the motives of the nonprofit are different than what he/she is used to. With the profit motive gone, a huge leverage tool is off the table. The motives behind a purchase are foreign to them as they are learning how to tie their products to the mission of the organization instead of to a profit motive. The next leverage tool they will use is the business efficiency line. That works for some sales and for some nonprofits, especially in the areas of finance where there is a great emphasis on auditing and accountability. However, most of the nonprofits I know will live a very long time with poor business processes, an excess of Excel spreadsheets running their business or an over-abundance of meetings and emails, before they decide to use a software solution to help them do their job better. A sales rep used to selling to the government will typically have the patience and relationship skills to sell to nonprofits, but is uncomfortable with the informality of the buying processes he/she encounters and isn't able to intuitively understand where the budget comes from for the projects he/she is trying to sell.

To successfully sell to a nonprofit I feel I must have the patience and relationship skills of someone who sells to the government, balanced by the discipline and skills of leading a prospect through a sale like a rep for for-profit companies. Why? For one, nonprofit organizations aren't usually organized, in the classic for-profit sense, in how they buy. That doesn't change the fact they must go through the same sales steps as any other type of sale, whether they know it or not, in order to feel comfortable at the time of the final closing of a sale. The other reason is, in a bizarre way, nonprofits have a disincentive to actually purchase a software solution. I want this point to sink in. Nonprofits do not necessarily have an incentive to make a purchase solution in the timeframe I, as a sales rep, hope they will.

A couple of the companies I have worked for were publicly-traded companies. Trying to get a nonprofit organization to buy something on our publicly-held company's fiscal quarter schedule can be a ridiculous conversation. The disincentive for many nonprofits to purchase is waiting another three months, six months, or twelve months won't make a huge dent in their mission and won't cost them the dollars against the expense category of their 990. If spending $100,000 at the end of your nonprofit's fiscal year meant you would go over your target expense-to-program ratio, my guess is you would postpone that deal even if it means that you push aside a couple of other deadlines. For reps used to selling the urgency of now, this can be maddening.

Nonprofits are budget-sensitive on all levels.

I'm pretty certain you are aware nonprofits live on a budget. Are we agreed on that point? I've had smart people ask me, in all honesty, how I could ever make a living selling something to a nonprofit. They forget to realize that nonprofit does not mean NO profit. It simply means that any profits made must be funneled back into the mission in a particular formula of expenditure. There are quite a few nonprofits out there with enormous budgets that stretch into the tens and hundreds of millions of dollars. I've always wondered if the business people who always say a nonprofit should act more like a business could have the return on their investment anywhere close to the program-investment-per-dollar-donated of most nonprofits, then we would have a great deal more profitable companies out there.

It is true, no matter the size and breadth of a budget of a nonprofit, they will be sensitive as to their spending on any and all levels. A hundred-million-dollar-a-year organization, for easy round numbers, most likely doesn't mean they have a huge pot of cash lying around to work on infrastructure projects for their business or marketing operations. Most likely a good portion of that budget comes from funding sources with strings attached or is already allocated to specific program needs, or other such items. If that nonprofit spends 15% of its $100,000,000 on infrastructure costs, where most license fees for software projects come from, then they really only have $15,000,000 to cover the cost of all of their building expenses, non-program covered employee expenses, utilities costs, insurance, and all of the other overhead that may be necessary.

I, in my sales role, have to be able to understand where the budget is and account for it being real in order for my management to be willing to marshal company resources for a sales process for a positive result and not for a wild goose chase. By having a conversation with your vendors about your budget sensitivity and availability it will help you weed out some vendors, have tough conversation with others, and allow others to add more resources for your search.

There are so many new ways to lose a deal when working with nonprofits.

I have seen nonprofits who contacted my company, in the best sincerity possible, ready to make a software choice and then, inexplicably, circumstances around their mission or funding come into play that can't be helped and things are called off. Houston, Texas, has been part of my territory for most of my sales career. I've spent a good deal of time there. I remember 2001 as a very difficult year to try to sell anything to nonprofits there. I had several solid opportunities working and then a trio of events happened that hurt funding for so many organizations for a good long while. Not only did they have the hard stop that was the economy after 9/11, but there was the natural disaster caused by Tropical Storm Allison which parked over the region and dropped thirty-seven inches of rain in June of that same year. Add to those two events the demolition of so much wealth from the collapse of Enron earlier that year and you have an economy that took a beating. Individual and corporate giving, what there was of it, went to the disaster-stricken, while the loss of Enron took out a great deal of the corporate giving and individual giving that came from the employees of that company.

All of these events had great effects on the businesses of the community. However, the nonprofits in the community, as you well know, always have a more difficult time in these situations. Those in need of your services expand and the funding in support of those needs does not. If you need more money for your program needs are you still likely to take that $100,000 and go buy and implement an expensive new piece of software no matter how much it is needed? Not likely. It is the nature of the beast. I couldn't have predicted 9/11, a tropical storm, or Enron, but each of these are unlikely instances that have a far deeper impact on nonprofit funding than on your typical business or governmental entity and, as such, means there are more unique ways and reasons I, in my sales role, can lose a deal.

Maybe it is external factors, maybe it is a board member who suddenly realizes a purchase is about to be made and then says he'll have his business do it for free (even though it is a subpar solution for the organization), or maybe it is a staffer or two who shouldn't have any role in the final decision, but are allowed to have a large one because of a weak consensus leadership decision-making model. These, and so many more, are reasons I have lost a specific deal in my sales career. I believe I have lost more deals to strange circumstances than I actually have to real competition. Each time I have tried to learn that one more nuance I need to check for, to remember to ask about, and to keep a lookout for in order to not get caught flat-footed again by a situation I was not prepared for. It is an awful feeling to have to go back to your VP of Sales and explain you lost a deal or had it postponed because of a situation you either didn't know about or weren't prepared for. Whatever the reason the deal falls away, even if it is clearly not anything you could have managed, the loss will always be viewed by your sales management as your fault because you clearly didn't have "control" over the sales process.

Every office I go into I look at the pictures on the desk, the books on the shelves, and the diplomas on the walls. Is their desk messy or clean, who do they mention they trust in the office? Any piece of information is valuable to understand how and why someone will make an ultimate decision about a product to be purchased. Sometimes I feel like a little spy, but knowing even the small details of the internals of an organization can be helpful in trying to sell to an organization. That's sales for you. You win a deal and everyone wants to share in the glory. You lose a deal and you generally suffer alone.

I know I've lost deals because of these and so many more various reasons....

- ☑ Some sort of internal fraud
- ☑ A pending lawsuit against or because of the nonprofit
- ☑ A change in funding from a state agency
- ☑ My champion leaving the organization for greener pastures right before they were going to sign the deal
- ☑ A board member's intrusion
- ☑ I was too big of a company and they wanted to work with a smaller, more personal company
- ☑ I was at a small company and they wanted to work with a larger, more established company
- ☑ The price was too high
- ☑ The price was too low. Seriously. They thought there was a catch.
- ☑ A natural disaster
- ☑ A terrorist attack
- ☑ A company decides to donate their employees' time to do the project instead
- ☑ Another company gave it away for dirt cheap to try to use that client as a reference site
- ☑ A staff member has a relative who knows a friend who can do some sort of tech programming and just got laid off

The list goes on and on and on. Many of these situations just plain do not exist in the for-profit world. To be successful selling to nonprofits I have to be prepared and ready for all of these and more strange scenarios. It's a good thing I like working with nonprofits like I do! In your daily work you can't prepare for many of these scenarios either. All we can do together is communicate expectations appropriately at the right time and control the situations we can control. Other than that, we can pray that there isn't a tropical storm or another Enron!

Formalize within the informality of the typical buying process.

A sales process, or a buying process for that matter, requires a bit of discipline to be successful. It doesn't have to be rigid and formal, but clear lines of what is and is not appropriate, helpful, and supportive to the overall effort of purchasing a sophisticated piece of software are needed. The vast majority of nonprofits I have dealt with can be fairly loose in their own organizational structures and, even if they do have a decent hierarchy, there are many unofficial dotted lines of authority the sales rep must begin to map and understand. After having mapped your organization's structure for who are the best contacts to talk to regarding their product the sales rep will cozy up with those folks in order to have a friendly ear in the right hallways. The determination of where the authority lies usually comes with a little help. We in sales talk about gaining a "champion" inside your organization. Each rep looks for a champion who can give them the inside look of an organization's politics. These relationships are well-cultivated to gain trust, acceptance, and knowledge. If a champion can't be found within the organization the next best thing is the consultant.

No matter the type of consultant employed, fundraising consultants, management consultants, board consultants, or other, a rep selling into an organization can find one that works with the organization who is helpful in learning what is needed to know more about in order to find a way in. If I can have the consultant become my champion then I can borrow a good bit of his/her organizational trust to have my product seen in a different light than the competition. The champions inside an organization will help overcome the most difficult part of selling to a nonprofit which is understanding who will ultimately be able to say yes to the solution and convince the others my solution is the right idea.

When I worked in the for-profit high tech field I would sell to companies that had very defined purchasing procedures. People at a certain level or position in a company typically had very exact amounts and types of purchases they were allowed to do. A strict power structure would be in place to keep purchasing restrictions in control. For example, a purchase to be made of $500,000 of software licenses would require a Director level approval, but $500,001 would require a Vice President approval unless, by contract, the vendor was approved for purchases without contract based upon prior relationship. As the sales rep, I would find out where these boundaries were and then utilize those lines to decide what type of discounts I would need to employ in order to allow the purchase to be signed off by a level of personnel where I had the best relationship. That way I had the path of least resistance to getting my software in the door and then growing that presence over time. Once in the door you become a current vendor to the company. That opens up quite a number of doors and opportunities to talk to people who would never have talked to you before. The second and third deals are always the opportunity to go after a much larger and company-wide deal since I was then a respected vendor to the company.

Clear lines of authority are not necessarily the standard case when it comes to decisions made within a nonprofit. These types of delineated roles don't necessarily work in a nonprofit management situation. This, I believe, comes out of the natural belief in inclusive decision making requiring consensus far more than ever happens in the for-profit business world. It is very hard for some new reps to the world of nonprofit selling to understand how to handle and manage the informal decision makers and the informal decision processes that happen. They are too accustomed to those rigid lines and set roles to handle selling to a nonprofit. If you get one of those kind of sales reps working with you it makes your ability to control the process from your side that much more important.

Understand the mission focus

The main way I learned to avoid losing deals, as best as possible, in all of the strange ways I have mentioned, is to make sure I am attuned to the mission focus of the organization. Understanding how the organization makes decisions and what the organization will need to buy can be summed up in the mission focus they have for themselves. All of the other items can happen -- long sales cycles, sensitive budgetary situations, strange ways to lose a deal, and different forms of buying processes-- and these can be overcome by having a keen understanding of the organization's mission and why it operates the way it does.

Sales reps, if they are astute, will look at everything they do with the mission of the nonprofit in mind. I have found that as long as I do that then I am able to overcome other obstacles and mistakes. The majority of people I have worked with at the numerous nonprofits I have been to can see when someone is truly interested and cares about the organization itself and is not just there to sell them something. In the for-profit world it is expected when the potential customer meets a potential vendor the sum total of the relationship between both parties is the value of the sale. For a nonprofit executive who cannot afford the cost, both psychologically and monetarily, of a mistake in a purchasing process, the sales relationship must offer more. It must offer a level of understanding, empathy, and partnership that does not always exist in the for-profit world of sales relationships.

Chapter summary:

The sales team that sells to a nonprofit must be able to understand and work within how the nonprofit world runs. To do that, one must study the sector and, hopefully, become a part of it. Though the sales cycles may be longer, budget sensitivity exists on all levels, many unique and different ways exist to lose a deal, and formal buying processes are not utilized internally, it all becomes worth it when I am able to match the mission of an organization to the benefits of the product I am selling.

Bringing it home:

- ☑ How long did it take you to manage your last buying process? Do you know why it took so long or was so quick?

- ☑ What type of vendor categories have you found yourself generally working with? Think of the four categories outlined in this chapter. How did any of the people in any category help or hurt your overall process?

- ☑ Take some time to talk with any consultants you work with and have a relationship level-set discussion with them to understand how they view working with you and with the vendors where they may have relationships.

- ☑ Does your organization have defined purchasing levels among your managers? Does that work for all types of purchases or does it change by type of purchase or the purchase's significance to the organization?

- ☑ Can you name the various members of your organization who were vital to your last large decision? Does their criticality in that process match their job title within your organization's structure? If not how and if so, did that help?

"Blake: We're adding a little something to this month's sales contest. As you all know, first prize is a Cadillac Eldorado. Anybody want to see second prize? [Holds up prize] Second prize is a set of steak knives. Third prize is you're fired."

From the movie Glengarry Glen Ross[6]

CHAPTER FIVE

Sales Stage	Percent to Sales Close	Stage Description
1	10%	Why This Matters
2	20%	The Nonprofit Buyer
3	30%	Unreliable Buying Techniques
4	40%	The Other Side of the Fence
5	50%	How a Sales Process Works on You
6	60%	Sales 101
7	70%	The Nonprofit Buyer Model of Control
8	80%	Adapting to your organization
9	90%	Closing the sale
10	100%	Deal done! On to the next one...

Salespeople can be an interesting group. It takes a special kind of person to live under the constant stress of a quota along with the pressures of making sure all of the working parts of a company work in unison to the benefit of a customer. Salespeople live and die by the numbers they are able to deliver for their company. That is a cold, hard truth. I tried to explain to my Dad once what being in sales is like. I explained it this way: Being in sales is like getting a yearly review every month.

There is pressure every month to produce the results and the numbers. I've been on sales teams where the sales numbers were placed on a wall every day for the team to see who was doing better than the other person. It was rough at times when I was the low man on the totem pole. It was great when I was on top. The pressure of that kind of results is not for everyone. Every salesperson at every vendor operates off of some sort of quota system where the sales numbers a rep brings in is important to their overall job security.

What I would like to do here is walk you through what I, as a sales rep, go through in trying to define my sales territory and how I try to understand the strategy I need to have to make my quota number. It all starts with the quota number which is always assigned by the company at the beginning of their fiscal year. A quota is how much I have to sell to keep my job that I love. In its simplest form it looks like this:

- ☑ **Sample Annual Quota:** $1,000,000 in software license revenue
- ☑ **Sample average software license sale:** $75,000
- ☑ **Number of average sales needed to get to quota:** 13.33 (of course a third of a sale isn't possible!)
- ☑ **3-4 x Quota Rule of thumb** - This is a standard rule of thumb that a sales pipeline should be 3 to 4 times your quota. That way, as deals ultimately fall in and out of your pipeline, there is a solid core of deals to rely on.

- ☑ **3-4 x quota** = $4,000,000
- ☑ **Number of deals I need to be actively following to make annual quota:** 40 or more
- ☑ **Number of prospects to touch to reach the 40 qualified prospects:** 400 (a 10x rule of thumb)

Those 40 potential sales are only in the pipeline because they have gone through a defined qualification process. That means there has to be a much larger number of potential targets out there, dubbed unqualified sales prospects, that have to be contacted via the various company marketing vehicles, relationship avenues, or plain old telemarketing (not fun, but necessary). I would typically say I need to touch ten times the number of prospects I need in order to make the three-to-four-times number. That means I have to have touched a whopping 400 nonprofits to find the forty that might be interested within the timeframe I have to sell something to satisfy quota and then try to work enough of those forty in order to get thirteen of them to actually buy something.

Definition of insanity

At that rate, if those numbers hold true, I have closed sales with roughly 2.5% of the nonprofits I have reached during that fiscal year. It can feel like an exhausting exercise of doing the same thing over and over and over again, but if it is done well then you never know if that next phone call, that next email, or that next tradeshow will bring you the contact you need to start the all elusive sales process with a qualified prospect. Time and again I have made that one extra phone call before or after hours and have been able to get a hold of the exec to restart a good sales process which may have been stalled before. Continuous discipline, quality relationship building, and utilizing the basic sales training techniques will generally ensure a sales rep is able to make that quota number. What I will do now is walk you through the process within which a sales rep will work to make that quota number a reality for them.

Pain, Budget, and Timeframe, oh my.

Blake: Put. That coffee. Down.
[pause]
Blake: Coffee's for closers only.
(Also from *Glengarry Glen Ross*)

Closing the deal is why, for a salesperson, one has a job and why one is able to keep that job. In the movie *Glengarry Glen Ross*, as base as it may be (it's rated R for language and lots of it), the sales reps in the room are told in point blank terms their job is to sell and sell alone. Nothing else matters. I have known people like that in my career. I'm not a fan of theirs. Selling, to me, isn't about winning. It's about the relationship. If the relationship isn't there, then the trust isn't there, and you won't get the sale and the referral for the next sale, and no one will be happy with their purchase at the end of the day.

Before I can even begin to think about the final close of the sale I have a great deal of work to do, work that starts with some very basic qualifying information. There are three basic components of qualifying information: Pain, Budget, and Timeframe. Does the prospect have a set of pains my solution could solve? Is there a project budget identified? When does the client want to get started with their project? These are basic questions that reveal much in the way of the nuances of the organization and how the sales process will move forward. Each salesperson you ever talk to will be trying to nail you down on these topics: Pain, budget and timeframe

- ☑ **Find the pain** - An organization must have some business process or application that is hurting them in how they try to do their daily business to even think about making a switch to a new system. Without a recognized pain the sales rep knows there will be little appetite for change. With nonprofit budgets being constantly squeezed, large scale applications, especially expensive ones, are not replaced willy-nilly. A typical financials application, for example, is only replaced roughly every seven years no matter the business pains inherent in the everyday use of the system. The pain of the software implementation can lead many to hold off for even more years than that before they make the next change. I've seen organizations go as long as twelve to fifteen years between major system upgrades. That is a long time in the world of technology and business reporting requirements. If the pain isn't great enough or felt keenly enough then there won't be any motivation for the organization to do something.

- ☑ **Find the budget** - Is a project already budgeted in the current fiscal year's budget, something for next year, or has a budget even been allocated yet? Is the money for the purchase coming from current funds, a grant, a large donor, government funds, or other sources? Add a currently authorized budget to a specified business pain and you are two-thirds of the way towards becoming a "qualified prospect." How about that?

- ☑ **Find out the timeframe** - As a sales rep you have to sell a certain amount of software within a certain period of time. The timeframe aspect is very important to the sales rep because, in a first-come-first-served world, the organization closest to making a decision will get the majority of my time and attention as well as whatever pre-sale resources I can bring to bear to help the organization. In a nutshell, I want to sell to those who are ready to buy now and keep those who have pain and budget, but later decision timeframes, in contact with me so they don't forget who I am and I can get to them later as they become ready.

There are multiple levels of data necessary for the vendor to gather beyond these three points obviously. We will get into all of these points in later sections of this book. As a nonprofit executive it is incumbent upon you to control how these core three items are communicated externally from the organization. Done incorrectly and you will setup a dysfunctional sales process from the get-go. Done correctly and you can set the tone for an orderly process that will get you accurate data from your vendors to help you make the right decision for your organization.

If you really want to learn some in-depth selling techniques, beyond the "Sales 101" that we will go through in the next chapter, I would recommend <u>The New Solution Selling</u> by Keith M. Eades[8] or <u>Proactive Selling</u> by William "Skip" Miller[9]. Both are good reads, but, for you, both will be far more informative than you might ever desire regarding the profession of sales. Each one, along with so many other sales "techniques" books out there, and there are as many of those as there are management books on how to be a better nonprofit, has its own unique points on how to do the job better. From <u>The New Solution Selling</u> book you will find this list of the basics of what a salesperson is supposed to do when they engage with a potential client. These are:

- ☑ Understanding your buyers, their situations and, most importantly, their needs
- ☑ Supplying mutually-defined solutions to your customers' recognized problems
- ☑ Gaining access to key decision makers
- ☑ Controlling the buying process
- ☑ Defining milestones that can be measured and forecasted

The first bullet point has always been my favorite, personally. The stereotype of a salesperson is a loud, extraverted talker. In reality, the best sales rep is the one who listens more than they talk. When I can be in a client discovery meeting and ask the right questions that has the client talk about their situation and needs for a good hour or more before I talk a lick about my company or product, then I'm doing a good job of listening. People like and appreciate the ability to share their pains. A good sales rep gives the potential customers the opportunity to do that. By doing so I learn a great deal about the organization and can begin working on bullet two, getting an idea of what solutions might work.

Notice one huge bullet point there-- the sales rep is taught to control the buying process. There are so many overt and covert strategies and tactics underneath that bullet point, but you must remember the vendors' team is attempting to steer you at every turn into activities that will support their potential sale. Even if, after our discovery discussions, I believe that the product I am selling will be a positive for your organization, it by no means belies the fact I am using our sales process to present the product to you in the best light possible.

This isn't a nefarious situation with plots being exercised from smoky back rooms. Controlling the process means simply trying to create a repeatable set of circumstances that will lead to a positive outcome for the work done. If, after those first discovery discussions, I make the realization my product is not a fit for your organization based upon the pain, budget, and timeframe requirements, then the conversation has to be had that says, "Thank you, but something else might be better for you." Not all sales reps will do that, however, and will try to find a way to fit a square peg into a round hole. That is why I will teach you how to control the process rather than having a process control you. Pain, budget, and timeframe...the first steps in the qualification process to start a sales process. How the salesperson manages that information gathering will go a long way to determining the type of sales relationship you will have with that particular vendor.

Ethical salespeople you ask? Is it possible?

There is an old salesperson joke that goes like this.....

How do you know the difference between a used car salesperson and a software salesperson?

Answer: The used car salesperson KNOWS when he is lying.

Funny to be sure, but there's always a kernel of truth in a joke. Your average salesperson out there does not know the intricacies of the product and is not expected to know such by his/her management. That is why there are sales engineers. The sales rep is there to try and manage the process, shepherd the company's resources properly, and foster the relationship with the client towards the closure of the sale. They are not there to know all of the ins and outs of the product and, honestly, can't know them all since it takes so much training time to learn some products. The people in a sales organization who know the product best are the sales engineers, implementation services team, and trainers. Get to know them as best you can.

The joke belies the fact that most, if not a vast percentage of, sales reps are honest people. Many are working with nonprofit organizations for some of the same desires, to give back and be a part of the nonprofit community as those who work at the nonprofit organizations themselves. There is a Russian proverb I remember hearing: "Trust but verify." A sales rep's job is to qualify the organization for a potential sale and to try to work the organization through the defined sales process towards that ultimate sale. How can you verify a sales rep you may not know to see if that person is ethical and will work with you on the level? Here are a few tips:

- ☑ Be careful of the salesperson who tries to be too technical
- ☑ Be careful of the salesperson who promises too much too quickly
- ☑ Keep track of promises and verify the information with the technical sales engineers or others
- ☑ Be careful of the sales rep who plays gatekeeper to others at the company too strictly for comfort
- ☑ Test the sales rep with specific follow-up. A sales rep who doesn't follow up on questions or promises is indicative of the potential relationship with the rest of the company.
- ☑ Get referrals to specific quality sales reps from other nonprofits you know that have purchased from that vendor

A good salesperson is your advocate within his/her company to help you find a win-win solution that will create a positive, long-term relationship between customer and vendor. Ethical salespeople are real and they do exist in every company. If you are getting a referral from a friend at another organization be sure to ask what their experience was with the sales team. That will tell you a great deal about the company itself.

Vendor seminars, product demonstrations, and on and on

Apart from your dealings with individual sales team members there will be other aspects of a sales process from a vendor that will attempt to be "touch points" with your organization. Typical touch points include vendor seminars, online webinars, trade shows, product demonstrations, whitepapers, press releases, and magazine reviews, which are all popular choices. Nowadays we can even add Facebook fan pages, online blogs, or Twitter updates to the list of ways companies attempt to get their message out and reel in interested potential clients. Each one of these sometimes seemingly benign events are carefully constructed tools designed to fit into specific sections of a sales process as designed by the vendor. Every time you are a part of one or more of these events you are, possibly unwittingly, adding yourself right into the vendor's database of potential prospects.

If you do download a whitepaper that asks you to register first, sign up to view a webinar, or even give your business card to a marketing person at a tradeshow always keep in mind what could be coming your way. Just as you may have a donor management program to keep track of all of the folks who give or could give to your organization, your vendors have extremely sophisticated software to track every interaction you have with them. Those interactions get scored and evaluated, and decisions are made about the type and depth of communication that the organization will seek with you. Sales reps will use these events and items as a way to bring you along with further information they know, according to their process, you should know prior to the designated next step they would like to work you into.

Accept each of these for what they are: sales process events. There will always be educational components to these sales steps, and they are designed to be that, but remember they are sales steps towards the end goal of closing the deal. As long as we are all clear about how these dance steps fit into our Vendor Dance then we are all clear about our role and how we can help each other along the way.

The voodoo of software licensing

The last line to cross in any sales process is always the price. Getting agreement on that will almost always require some type or series of negotiations. Pricing is such a sensitive subject, especially for nonprofit organizations. And let's face it -- software licensing is a big pain in the... Trust me; it is from the vendor's point of view, too.

Every vendor has specific reasons as to why they price items the way they do. Even to those who work for that vendor the reasons as to why could seem murky at best. I envision a vendor executive with a myriad of spreadsheet cost models in front of him/her as he/she wonders how many deals he/she has to sell in order to pay for the business and if I just charge X more per deal then I only need this many deals to pay for the business and ten more than that and we can afford the next round of growth. Then once all of the spreadsheets and numbers start to form into one ugly mass he/she must pull out his/her voodoo spell book, turn to the chapter on how to price software, and do his/her thing. At least that's what it can seem like. No matter the logic once explained it always still feels like they made it up.

The software licensing employed by a company is also a sales tactic. Many sales teams do not wish to even talk pricing, show a pricing spreadsheet, or give out a potential price until much later in a buying process. If you ask early on in the process you may get the dreaded words from a software salesperson of, "Well, it depends." The truth is that, in many cases, it actually does depend on so many factors that haven't even entered into the discussion yet, but a bad pause and those dreaded words are sure to strike budgetary fear into any potential client. Whole sections of sales trainings are devoted on how to answer that first pricing question in the manner the company wants it answered. The exact verbiage becomes very important.

Companies seem to vary between two basic formulas for software pricing. It's either an all you can eat type of solution or a granular/modular approach. One is supposed to give you extra value and less confusion while the other is supposed to give you options to pick and choose what you actually need. Unfortunately, it can all just become confusing, especially when you are trying to compare apples to apples among vendors.

For a vendor, profitability is all about the right licensing schema which produces the necessary form of maintenance and support revenue that provide the predictable revenue that allows a company to plan staffing, future code development, and essential business functions. For any publicly-traded software company you will see this type of revenue broken out in specific line items on their financial reports and it is how they are judged as financially healthy by every financial analyst out there. To understand licensing you have to understand maintenance and support. Most companies won't negotiate maintenance and support. They may discount the heck out of licensing, but will insist on maintenance and support to be at specific levels. This may be a requirement of specific legalese because of revenue recognition rules required by the IRS, but beyond that most maintenance and support is extremely high profit in the software industry.

Some rules to live by about software licensing:

- ☑ Be careful of licensing based on usage statistics. They almost always end up causing issues later on, though the numbers may look good upfront.

- ☑ Negotiate maintenance and support charges, especially during implementation periods. The price may not change, but when you have to pay it might.

- ☑ Products can get bundled into another name making them ineligible for maintenance upgrades. Ask what falls under a maintenance plan and what doesn't, especially for main version upgrades.

- ☑ Research potential promos or competitive application switch discounts - a not-so-great sales rep may not, unfortunately, tell you about them if he/she thinks he/she can sell the product to you without using them.

- ☑ Get the vendors to help you compare apples to apples if it starts getting confusing. Realize you may not ever get to an actual apples-to-apples discussion because of the vast differences in the details in what you are looking at between the vendors' systems.

- ☑ Don't let the pricing discussions feel awkward to you. The price of the deal has to match the value you will experience. Have that discussion with the vendor if something doesn't seem right to you.

Chapter summary:

Being in sales can be an interesting, enjoyable, fun, and unique career. It does take a bit to get used to making a living on a quota. The constant pressure of the numbers is something that, quite honestly, I have to put in the background of mind. If I don't, I begin to worry more about the number than I do worry about the customer. That is a recipe for failure. My experience has shown me, if I am able to do right by the potential customer, then the numbers take care of themselves. By taking care of the customer I mean focusing on the key information to make sure there is a real "fit" between what the customer needs and what I have to offer, by being an ethical person in all of my dealings, and dealing honestly when it comes to cost and our resource availability.

This chapter explored the beginning of the sales side of the process. I wanted to make sure you understood why your salespeople were asking you certain types of questions and how certain standard vendor activities brought you into their sales world. Every conversation, every marketing event or piece, every phone call and demo, and even the pricing negotiation are tactics/techniques within a sales process. Most of you, I know, realize these are sales events intended to influence you, but the step we will discuss a little later is how to turn that knowledge to work for your organization.

Bringing it home:

- ☑ Remember a time where you attended a vendor event and were impressed with the follow-up that was done afterwards. Did it match your expectations? How did it make you feel about the vendor, positively or negatively?

- ☑ Think through your pricing negotiations you have had with various vendors. What worked best to make a pricing situation clear for you to be able to compare one product to another? What was frustrating for you about a vendor's pricing?

- ☑ List the top two or three best and worst salespeople and vendors you have dealt with over time. What were the common characteristics of each in how they worked with you?

"Let the watchwords of all our people be the old familiar watchwords of honesty, decency, fair-dealing, and commonsense."
President Theodore Roosevelt
New York State Fair, Syracuse, September 7, 1903

CHAPTER SIX

Sales Stage	Percent to Sales Close	Stage Description
1	10%	Why This Matters
2	20%	The Nonprofit Buyer
3	30%	Unreliable Buying Techniques
4	40%	The Other Side of the Fence
5	50%	How a Sales Process Works on You
6	60%	Sales 101
7	70%	The Nonprofit Buyer Model of Control
8	80%	Adapting to your organization
9	90%	Closing the sale
10	100%	Deal done! On to the next one...

Sales is an art and a science. It's an art because there are nuances to the relationship-building that can never be codified. It is science because they are codified steps that, if not followed properly, and experience shows this to be true, will make the end of a potential sale clumsy and prone to failure. This chapter is to give you a taste of what those codified steps are like and what those sales books teach those salespeople who are calling on you. The goal of this book, of course, is not to teach you to become a sales rep. Rather, this chapter, with the sales training information in it, is intended to give you the background basics of how the sales team at the vendor works and how that then relates to their interactions with you.

There has been a great deal of effort undertaken by sales teams to make the art of relationships in a sales process into as much of a science as possible. I will say that many of the repeatable steps I learned early in my sales career during what I thought were interminable sales training classes have served me well. I remember a two-day sales training session while I worked for Unison Software, a company later acquired by IBM. The company had put us up in a conference room on the top floor of the old Hilton in Austin, Texas. A great view of the city was the best distraction as the sales trainer, a self-described, Jesuit-educated former Marine took us through some ungodly number of PowerPoint slides. He was bound and determined to go through every single slide no matter how fast he had to talk. I had one of those moments during that session that surprises you that you remember it, but sums up the whole experience quite well. I was on a quick break and saw out the window the annual Austin SpamFest (yes, we have one of those in Austin along with numerous other festivals) and thought how much I'd rather be judging the spam sculpture contest than sitting in that conference room. My dream of becoming a spam sculpture judge dashed, I stayed in the training for the full term. I will admit I even learned a thing or two.

This diagram should look familiar to you from the opening of each chapter. This chart, however, adds in a fairly standard definition of what is actually expected from the sales reps as they move a prospect through a sales process and ultimately to a closed sale. Each stage is defined by a specific milestone. This is, by no means, a definitive look at how every sales team maps out their stages. Variations on a theme for these stages change as fast as the direction of the wind out on the plains, but you will find something similar to this in almost every sales organization known to man.

Sales Stage	Percent to Sales Close	Stage Description
1	10%	Progress from Interest to Initial Action
2	20%	Need to Buy Outlined by Prospect
3	30%	Vendor is Compelling Solution to Prospect
4	40%	Coach at Suspect Agrees Vendor is Compelling Solution
5	50%	Prospect Decision Makers Agree on Vendor
6	60%	Pricing is Agreed Upon
7	70%	Prospect States Desire to Go with Vendor
8	80%	Discussions on Steps to Close Sale
9	90%	Contractual and Logistical Issues Put to Rest
10	100%	Sale Closed!

As we've discussed in the previous chapter, being in sales is about numbers. There are specific pieces of information a sales rep will try to gain at the beginning of a sales process (pain, budget, and timeframe as described earlier in this book) and initial buying techniques, like RFP or discovery sessions, to gain information about your organization. These are all just the beginning of what is involved in a sales process. If you have run a sales process to purchase software in the past you may have set up a quality set of buying steps in order to be in control of the situation. The reality is you probably were not in control from the first point of contact. That isn't an indictment of you at all. It only means from that first point of contact, sales reps are trained to try to take control of the sales process and turn you down their specific road. Whether it is the information they send, the references they have you contact, or how they answer the questions in the RFP, it all comes down to a model of controlling the sales process.

If a sales rep manager doesn't feel the rep is managing the process for a particular prospect well, the manager will ask for a sales plan with specific activities that the rep is going to use to guide the prospect through to lead the prospect to the positive decision they both hope for. When a sales rep loses a deal there is generally a postmortem to try and understand where the process got away from him/her and what could have been done differently in order to win the business.

This model for control, at some sales organizations, goes all the way down to specific phrases and verbiage in how to explain products. These phrases will be market-focus tested to ensure they are conjuring up the right images when they are spoken to a particular group of sales targets or person of a specific job title. Speaking of job titles, you will hear salespeople or other marketing types talking about "C-level" contacts. They are referring to executive level positions such as **CEO, CFO, CIO, COO**, etc. A sales rep tries to find out how to get a conversation with the right member of this executive team as early on in the sales process as possible. The stats I have seen over the years clearly state the earlier in the process the sales rep is able to get into discussions at the C-level at a nonprofit, or any other type of sales for that matter, the more likely they are to win that business. Fact of life right there. One more reason for you to understand: a conversation is not just a conversation. They all have deeper psychological meanings whether you want to believe it or not. Huge dollars are spent on the psychology of each specific conversation in a sales process and how to get each exact point across at the right time.

The next two charts are sample sales process diagrams that display the roles, process steps, tasks, and tools available to a sales rep during the sales process. These are pulled together from several different examples I have worked with at different sales departments over the years.

The first diagram illustrates how many people can be involved with you during your sales and delivery cycles with a vendor. According to this chart we have twelve different people doing their job within seven different process stages. To understand this diagram read down the left to see who the various individuals at the company that are included in the sales process as well as the goals and outcome of each process stage. Read across the top for the main sections of their sales process. Intersect the two sides to see who owns what part of that specific section of the process and even what time commitment is expected of the other players at that exact time.

Sales Process Stages, Roles, Responsibilities, Goals

Sales Process Stages, Roles, Responsibilities, Goals, Tasks, and Tools

Responsibility Within Each Process Section
1 = Own Process Section
2 = Lead Process Section
3 = Contribute to Process Section
4 = None

Expected Time Commitment Within Each Process Section
Dedicated
Significant
Minimal
None

	Sales Process Stage						
	Territory Planning	Early	Middle	End	Decision	Delivery	Value Attainment
Goal of Stage	Plan short/long term approach for sales in territory	Gain agreement on potential value at account	Gather business/IT issues, pain points, goals, strategy	In-depth value solution developed. Eval process?	Get signed order from the customer	Deliver the solution	Validate the customer receives value. Position for next solution.
Customer Moved to Next Stage Upon	Account plan and action plan complete	Customer agreement of problem that we can potentially solve	Understand all business and IT drivers/goals. Customer desires proposal.	Requirements/objections managed, financial value/business link confirmed?	Customer Order	Customer Implemented successfully	Customer reference
Sales Process Role							
Sales Representative	1	1	2	2	1	3	3
Technical Sales Engineer	3	3	3	3	3	3	3
Partner Development Mgr	3	2	3	3	3	4	4
Subject Matter Expert	4	4	3	1	3	3	1
Contract and/or Legal Dept	4	3	4	3	3	3	3
Solutions Delivery Team	3	3	1	2	3	3	3
Implementation Consultant	3	3	3	2	3	3	3
Services Sales Executive	3	3	3	3	3	3	3
Post-Sales Project Manager	3	3	3	2	3	1	2
Post-Sales Architect	4	4	4	3	3	3	2
Post-Sales Consultant	4	4	4	4	4	2	3
Customer Support	4	4	4	3	3	3	3

In this next diagram we continue the stages of the previous diagram, but add to it the various tasks and tools involved in each of those stages. Follow the stages across the top and intersect to the column on the left to see what typical task or tool is commonly employed at the various process stages. These are just quick samples. It can get even more detailed than these diagrams I assure you!

Sales Process Tasks and Tools Necessary per Process Stage

	Territory Planning	Early	Middle	End	Decision	Delivery	Value Attainment
Tasks	Develop Strategic Account Plan	Gather Business Drivers, Objectives, Opportunities	IT Business Process and Maturity Assessments	Develop Solutions Architecture	Finalize Business Case	Create Implementation Roadmap	Value Realization
	Develop Services/ Partner Strategy	Deliver Value Messages	Value Definition	Custom Demos	Proposal with Statement of Work Delivered	Program Definition	Customer Support
		Preliminary Value Calculation	Delivery Custom Briefings	Proof of Concept if Required	Final Task Review (Legal, Revenue Estimation)	Value Measurement	
		Update Services/Partner Strategy		Custom Financial Projection	Negotiation of Final Deal	Project Execution	
		Conduct Basic Briefings		Solution Design and Delivery Estimates		Customer Support Communication/ Escalation	
				Executive Business Case Development			
				Customer Support Planning/ Escalation			
Tools	Regional Territory Planning Templates	Brainstorming	Assess Current Capabilities of Customer	Custom Demos Support	Executive Business Case Templates	Standardized Delivery Methodology	Benefits Assessment Meeting
	Account Planning Templates	Value Blueprint	IT Business Assessment	Financial Justification Calculator	Best Practices Support	Benefits Measurement Templates	
			Sector Templates	Solution Proposal	Reference Visits		
			Potential Value Calculator	Benefits Definition Workshop			
			Gap Reports	Value-based Demos			

Impressive isn't it? The vendor knows exactly what people they want involved with you at a specific stage of their sales process because they have spent the time and money to map their past successes and are attempting to make their sales process as much of a predictable and repeatable process as possible. Not all pieces of these diagrams are always done or done in this exact order, but if one is not done it is up to the sales rep to justify why the next step resources are ok to be utilized. If that justification is not acceptable the sales rep will be asked to go back and grab some "control" over the process as moving the client forward without the required data will only end up causing problems later. Make sense?

All of the process steps in the world do not mean much if there isn't an agreement that the goals and pains of the client don't match a particular product fit of your vendor. Next is a typical "Discovery Map" which shows how a sales team will decipher your project goals and pains into specific sections. If the goals and pains do not align here then any thought of moving forward with the prospect will be questioned heartily.

Sample Opportunity Discovery Map

Goals	Maintain current funding level or grow funding level				
	Demonstrate strong fiscal accountability. Ensure funding sources are not at risk.				
Business Pains	No consistent method for pre-award internal analysis	Takes too long to get a consolidated financial view	Not effectively managing vendors	Grant management reports are not timely and often inaccurate	No visibility across vendors
	Cannot evaluate pre-award proposals historically	Multi-currency financial activity making it difficult to consolidate financials	Data not consistent across organization	Cannot accurately report time and effort expended against a specific grant	
Technical Pains	No tools to help manage pre-award proposal process	Exchange rate fluctuations are difficult to manage	Each field office using their own solution	Cannot connect to all remote country offices	Cannot track or process indirect costs related to each grant.
Product Positioned	Grant Management	Foreign Currency Management	Fund Accounting Management	Data Replication	Grant Management

There isn't a set timeframe for how long each stage of a sales process should last. Each sales team will have their own set of cultural norms for how long an organization is allowed to be reported at one stage before the sales rep is questioned on it and asked to move them up or down on their chart. Since you now know how you may be boxed into a sales tracking program you can utilize that to your advantage by having a blunt conversation with your sales rep to discuss where that rep thinks you are in his process, tell him where you believe you are, and then tell that rep what he/she could do for you to feel that you are ready to move to their next step.

See that? You just took a little bit of control back.

Before I move on and talk about how a sales team is organized, paid, and so forth I thought you'd like to see how your organization is placed into boxes and matched to the various needs of each person involved. The whole idea of a "model of control" is to understand your organization better than you know yourself. Each piece of your nonprofit is dissected for importance and influence towards the vendor goal of the sale.

Sales teams organizations

Sales teams are both highly uniform and highly specialized organisms. Most sales organizations from company to company look remarkably the same. The process for what team member does what within that vendor may be very different depending upon what that vendor sells to the marketplace. You can, however, bet most are going to be pretty similar. There is a marketing department trying to find new sales prospects, or leads, through various mechanisms such as trade shows, mailers, webinars, seminars, or telemarketing. There is a sales team responsible for guiding the qualified "prospect," not a lead anymore, through the various sales steps necessary for the organization to make a decision, utilizing several internal resources (technical, legal, executive) along the way. Lastly, there is an implementation team of some kind to make sure the software is installed, training is properly delivered, and the customer is ultimately satisfied with their purchase.

A sales team is setup in such a way that the further you go along in the sales process the more resources from the company you will be afforded. Resources are treated as a scarcity in all sales organizations in order to see that those who are deemed the best sales prospects are given timely access to the resources needed. Those deemed unqualified prospects or whose purchasing decisions are pushed off a few months will be gently guided to other less personnel-intensive resources until they get closer to their decision date. These resources are controlled by the sales rep. As a sales rep, it is my job to be the steward of all company resources and I am judged on my ability to not waste my time or anyone else's. When a great deal of time and resources are spent on what turns out to be a non-qualified prospect, because I didn't ask the right questions to know if the organization was a qualified prospect or not, then there is grief to pay all the way up the food chain and it is not fun.

Sample Sales Team Organizational Chart

CEO				
VP of Marketing	**VP of Sales**		**Implementation Services**	**Support**
Lead Generation	Sales Managers	Partner Development Manager	Implementation Services Manager	Level One Support
Events	Sales Reps	Business Development Manager	Project Manager	Support Escalation
Marketing Communication	Technical Sales Managers		Project Architect	Development Support
	Technical Sales Team		Project Consultant	

As a targeted organization you may arrive into the sales process with your vendor in any number of ways. It could be via an event, a mailer, a telemarketing call, or just a relationship with a sales team member. Once in, you will probably talk with a sales team member first. That sales team member will begin his/her line of questioning, or qualification. If certain questions are answered in specific ways and the sales rep sees specific circumstances which would warrant bringing in other team member specialties then you will start to meet other members of the team. Those other members would start with some sort of technical salesperson, a product specialist of some kind, and then, if you get closer to needing estimates on implementation services, you would start to meet members of the implementation services team. This is a simple example to give you an overall lay of the land in terms of the types of people you will be dealing with.

Remember, in dealing with a sales organization your technical members of the team and, to some extent, the marketing team are all trained to avoid discussing any kind of pricing. That is always funneled to the salesperson who is the only person authorized to discuss the pricing of the software or a services engagement. This is done very purposefully. It is to ensure the most sensitive part of the discussion is done with one voice.

The sales process chart, as illustrated earlier, is a good one for you to see how certain parts of a vendor company are expected to interact with you, the customer, at the various parts of your relationship with a vendor. As you can see, the definitions can get quite complex with defined roles for specific sections of a sales process and specific actions and agreements to get at each stage. The intent for showing these types of charts to you is for you, as a buyer, to understand there is a method to the madness and what you can expect from a sales organization you are in contact with about a potential purchase. I want you to see the kind of resources sales teams pull together to in order to showcase their products to you.

For further clarification of the various sales team definitions and roles, see Chapter "100% Deal done! On to the next one..." I think you will find the team outlines interesting. Does this make a little more sense now? There is a little logic in this madness. Despite the varying types of products you might be looking into, the sales teams you will be dealing with are going to be remarkably similar in scope, personnel, incentives, and roles. Knowing each of these roles, what makes each one tick, and how to work that to your advantage or to cut through the bluster where possible will help your organization make a better decision when the time comes.

Still about the numbers, aka the Urban General Fund

The Urban General Fund is what my wife and I affectionately call our own personal bank account. It's great to be able to allocate more dollars to that fund each month! There are many headaches to being in sales. However, if you do well, you are compensated for it. Sales reps selling to for-profit big corporations definitely make more money than sales reps selling to nonprofit organizations, but it is still a decent living if you can make it.

Companies with one or a hundred salespeople always try to design compensation plans that promote specific company goals. Those goals could be to sell more services, to prop up a particular product mix that has been lagging, or to try and get sales to come in during specific calendar timeframes. These compensation plans, typically at least 50% of a salesperson's overall compensation, can get so complicated in all of the micro-managed goals the company is trying to promote that it is impossible to try to do it all in the way the company wants.

When I was at Dell, my first sales job out of college, I learned a valuable lesson about quota. I was selected out of my team for a KIT lunch. KIT stood for Keep In Touch and was a way for senior management to hear from us little people. It was actually a fascinating lunch for a new salesperson who, at the time, still didn't intend to make a career out of sales by any stretch of the imagination. The Senior VP of Sales who moderated the discussion during lunch said a company's job is to create a comp plan that incents the salesperson to sell to the company goals and, on the flip side, it is the job of the salesperson to try to use the comp plan to try to make as much money as possible despite the stated company goals. If the salesperson could make more money within the comp plan by going against the stated company goals then the company screwed up. This was indeed an interesting statement from the head of worldwide sales at Dell at the time. I've used this statement over and over again throughout the years as a means to try and keep management from making comp plans that are overly complex. The more complex they are the more a sales rep will find a way to beat the system in order to make a better comp result for his/her own family General Fund.

Kintera, for example, had a revenue model that made a percentage off of the online credit card transactions its clients had from within its system. In the early days of the company these transaction percentages were seen as what would be the main revenue for the company. Later on, that panned out to not to be the case and monthly license fees became more and more important. The early comp plans incented the sales rep to sell deals that were heavy on transaction percentages and light on monthly license fees. Several sales reps were able to take advantage of that early focus, and the commission structures that came with it, to sell large transaction-based clients. They made very good money for several years by selling to a comp plan that did not help the company in the long term. They didn't do anything wrong, of course. They sold to the company goals. Unfortunately, the company goals were a tad flawed. It did help the company on one level. The company was able to quickly gain a large client base of recognizable brand names around the country that proved invaluable at getting other non-early adopter organizations to try out Kintera. It did not help the company get to profitability though.

One phrase you will hear in sales circles is that sales reps are "coin-operated." Put a quarter in and you get a benefit out of the machine. It is true to some extent. A good portion of a sales rep's compensation, not to mention his/her job security, is based around the commission and quota plan. If I, as a rep, am spending too much time on activities that do not lead to quota-relieving sales, then I've shot myself in the foot. I'm not doing myself any favors because I'm not doing activities that will help me in my core job function, help me to get paid, or also keep me in the job I enjoy. I do not consider this an excuse to blow off people you are talking to who say they are not going to be buying for a number of months. Every contact and every person is very important. Every sale, however large or small, had better have equal value in the eyes of your rep. A good sales rep will work with you cheerfully and deliberately no matter the occasion, but if you truly are not a qualified prospect you will be directed to the right part of the sales team for your next round of communications. The relationships are important, critical mind you, but my time is the first and foremost thing I can manage in order to hit my quota number.

In a buying process it wouldn't hurt you to talk to your sales rep, if you feel like you have a good relationship with him/her, about his/her compensation and how your sale could affect that. Work with them on getting an extra discount to have a deal come in during a timeframe important to the company. See if there is a way you could add some extra product to up the price of the deal in exchange for some other concession that will help the rep reach a percentage break on the commission. There are many ways you could ultimately help each other. Without the right relationship with your sales rep your request to talk about this kind of material may come off as crass or rude. Tread lightly unless you feel you have either been given an opening to have that kind of discussion or know the person well.

For definitions of how a sales rep is paid and common jargon surrounding that, see Chapter "100% Deal done! On to the next one..." Those terms will help you when you have the money/cost discussion with your vendor.

Verbiage is important

This is the last piece of our Sales 101 training. This section isn't about organization or motivation, but is about messaging. When I am learning a product or solution I work to get down specific phrases that will fit in various sales situations I will find myself in. I memorize a ten-second, thirty-second, one-minute, and five-minute outline of my company and my solution that I can pull out in any random place I may find myself in where I have a chance to communicate a strict message. More than a few times I've ended up in an elevator, in a break room, or on a trade show floor where I have needed to use these or combinations of these exercises to talk with folks I have wanted to make an introduction to. I take it all the way to what few second slogans or phrases will capture interest if I am calling up someone cold on the phone or sending emails I am hoping to get a reaction from. Every specific phrase and slogan you see from a company has most likely been tested and argued over before it ever reaches your ears.

I thought it would be helpful for you to see an outline of a very light sales script. Most standard telemarketing scripts are very rigid with specific questions and if/then scripts based upon the answers you give in the conversation.

Sales teams are taught to memorize these and such scripts about their company and products. Once you get the right person on the line you know you only have a short period of time to let them know you have a positive reason for them to listen to you. As such, your first words had better be good. In a call like this the statistics will show a sales rep has only seconds to capture someone's attention before that person tunes you out and are looking for a way to get off the phone. So make the first impression count.

One last quick note...most leads today for a vendor are not found through the traditional "cold call" where a rep is blindly calling down a list hoping to get someone on the phone to talk to about their product. Most leads are follow-ups from various activities as mentioned, email or direct mail inquiries and so forth. How "warm" or "cold" the lead may be does not diminish the need to have the script and message down to accurately portray your company in a concise period of time.

Outline of a basic script for a sales call

- Determine main and alternate contacts
- Search in all available information sources (database lists, website)
- If main contact is not available work down the list beginning at C-Level to gain a contact
- Manage the gatekeepers
    - When asked what the call is regarding provide name, company, and short value statement.
    - If asked to leave a message get the best name to contact and a time that would be best to call back.
- If reach contact
    - Introduce yourself and give company name

- ☑ Be polite by asking for and respecting their time.
- ☑ If the person is not your main contact ask the person if there is a better person to talk to after you have given your company overview/value statement.
- ☑ Keep in mind that you will have 30-60 seconds to get your point across before the contact will want to move on from the call.
- ☑ Have company overview/value statement practiced and ready because the idea is to lay context and gain interest traction quickly.
- ☑ Key messages
    - ☑ 3-5 key "why this call" points - If made it past initial company overview/value statement then begin to work in the 3-5 key points as to why this call is being made and why their organization should learn more about our company.
    - ☑ Positioning statement - Insert 2-3 main positioning points against competition.
- ☑ Points to learn in call
    - ☑ Each type of call has different standard information to gather to help aid the sales effort. Have the list of questions written out and ready to insert into the conversation.
- ☑ Goal of first intro call
    - ☑ The goal of this call could be one of two things: A phone call is set up to gather deeper interest and needs or an appointment in one of the cities/regions that we are trying to visit and do multiple appointments.
- ☑ First call should be no longer than 10-20 minutes in length. If getting close to that time, thank the person for their time and work to arrange the follow up call.
- ☑ Follow up to the call
    - ☑ Set up next call with internal resources.
    - ☑ Use the standard email script with sample documents to email as a thank you note.

If you have been on the receiving end of a call that follows an outline such as this then this may sound familiar. Just like the overall sales process itself, individual scripts for certain sections of the process are tested for their ability to bring about the desired results.

Chapter summary:

Am I a Sales Rep now? This was your brief intro to Sales 101. If you want to know how to take control of your own buying process I believe it is important to understand those who are attempting to impose a sales process on you, what their motivations are, how they are organized, and why they are saying what they are saying. Moving on from here we will take the sales knowledge you have learned and the characteristics of the people you are dealing with every day and put it into the context of your own Nonprofit Buyer Model of Control.

Bringing it home:

- ☑ Have you ever felt comfortable enough with a sales rep to have a blunt conversation with him/her about where you feel you are within his/her sales process and why? Why not or, if so, how did it help or change your relationship with that rep?

- ☑ In your current or your previous buying processes were you able to clearly see how the vendor allocated resources for you during the process? Did that allocation seem natural or did you have to force the issue to have access to certain parts of the vendor in order to have your questions answered?

- ☑ Have you ever talked with a sales rep about their compensation and how your sale could affect that? Was it uncomfortable or helpful? Why or why not?

- ☑ What are the most positive or negative experiences you have had with a cold or warm sales call from a vendor? How did those first touches from the vendor affect your impression of them as a whole?

"If you are prepared, you will be confident, and will do the job."
Tom Landry
Head Coach of the Dallas Cowboys for 29 years

CHAPTER SEVEN

Sales Stage	Percent to Sales Close	Stage Description
1	10%	Why This Matters
2	20%	The Nonprofit Buyer
3	30%	Unreliable Buying Techniques
4	40%	The Other Side of the Fence
5	50%	How a Sales Process Works on You
6	60%	Sales 101
7	70%	The Nonprofit Buyer Model of Control
8	80%	Adapting to your organization
9	90%	Closing the sale
10	100%	Deal done! On to the next one...

Let's see...to this point in our journey together here we have walked through a good deal of what it is like out there for salespeople and their targets, what is wrong with certain buying procedures commonly used by nonprofits, how a sales process works on you in your nonprofit, learned a little bit of what it is like to be a sales rep who is trying to sell to you(!), and now we are going to spend some time coalescing how we might be able to do this process together a little better.

I want to make sure you are in a position to have a new kind of sales relationship with your vendors. Every vendor you talk to has their own "model of control" for their sales process so you can consider this your very own model of control. Your Nonprofit Buyer Model of Control consists of these four points:

- ☑ **CBIs** - Definition of your very own Critical Business Issues, the high level reasons your organization needs to make a particular purchase.

- ☑ **Organization Outline** - Definition of your organization's mission, users of all sorts who might need access to the system you are researching, and the like.

- ☑ **Return on Mission** - Explanations of how you expect your purchase to impact the mission of the organization.

- ☑ **Doable Logistics** - A nice explanation for the vendor as to your timeframe, budget, and communication process during the sale along with other good relationship expectations.

With these four points in mind you will be able to come to your buying process from a position of control. The vendors coming your way will be presented a wealth of incredibly helpful and useful information. Together, you and the vendors will be able to quickly determine if your organization fits in their sweet spot for a potential sales opportunity and should be pursued further thus saving everyone time and energy. You will be able to rule out much of the guesswork and back-and-forth conversations at the beginning of a process that happens until one or the other decides the situation isn't a match and shouldn't be pursued. If you remember the "Vendor Dance" discussion then the information you have would be like setting up the perfect online dating profile.

Successful nonprofit looking for long-term relationship seeks vendor who is stable, profitable, and easy to work with. Must understand me, listen to my needs, and have quality references that will tell me the good and bad. Turnoffs are arrogant know-it-alls, high maintenance and support costs, and unknown fix-it charges.

With this model of control you will get to be the one to set the tone and tenor of the discussions. The right vendor will appreciate your preparedness and be excited to work with someone ready to go. This vendor will, undoubtedly, bring some quality suggestions to the table based on their experiences with other like customers, but will be glad to see how much skin you have in the game from the beginning. The wrong vendor will probably try to tell you how all or most of your assumptions are wrong and how they can do it all better for you. As Yoda might say, trust your feelings. You know you better than anyone.

What we cannot change with your Nonprofit Buyer Model of Control is the ease of which you are able to find all of the potential vendors that could be of help to you. That will still require a good deal of work on your part to scour the internet and various resources high and low for potential vendors. As always, a great resource is your own list of professional contacts. Ask others you know about their positive and negative experiences with various vendors. Those are always great as they are generally honest to a fault as opposed to many vendor-provided references who may just tell you their positive experiences.

Lastly, you may have noticed none of the above criteria for your model of control list out the technical requirements for a system. It is my opinion, and one shared by many of the experts in information technology, too much time is spent worrying about the technology infrastructure ahead of the business needs that must be solved. To be clear, before any technical infrastructure needs should be taken into account, you must research systems that fit your business needs first. Once the business needs are determined to be met by several applications then the merits of the various technical infrastructures the products deploy can be taken into account. At least by then you will know each of the applications you are reviewing will match your CBIs and you will have your choice of application that will fit your specific IT resources you can bring to the table. Don't rule out any solutions based on technical infrastructure alone. Vendors who have the right business solution for you will try to find a way to work with you if they can, even if you can't support the technical needs of their application. The right vendor will be upfront with you with regard to any non-standard options that are available.

Now that is out of the way, let's dive into your Nonprofit Buyer Model of Control.

Point one: Defining your critical business issues

Everything you do should start with the high level reasons as to why you need to make a specific purchase. Purchasing always starts with the pains involved and that are felt deeply within the organization. The first trap is to start thinking, "How in the world can I figure this out? I must need to hire a consultant. I don't have time to figure this out." It's easy to think that way because the purchasing process can be intimidating and you want to get it right. I like to think of it this way. You've all done this process before on a larger level. You have, no doubt, spent many days and hours in meetings deciding how to express the mission of your organization. Once that was done you spent the next set of days and hours working on the strategic pieces needed to make that mission successful. From there you started on the tactics that would get you there. I've been in these meetings and they can be great or they can be interminable. Thankfully, the ones I've been in have been well-led and productive I believe. Now, for your new application, just translate that process into a new direction.

Start with the over-arching organizational pains you are having. What business or communication processes are breaking down that are causing you issues in delivering on your program, getting accurate and timely data to your funders, difficulty in fundraising execution, and so forth? Examples are always a great way for us visual-learning types so let's walk through a quick one:

A medium-sized organization is struggling under an older accounting system purchased over ten years ago. They have grown from one main office environment to multiple program locations over the years. In that time their funders have also changed how they track their particular programs and want more granular data on key program statistics. The old "buckets of data" that used to suffice for reporting purposes no longer give them the right data to detail for their funders much less for their auditors under the new IRS 990 rules. As they have grown they have also seen spikes in employment costs, and management of time sheets for paid and volunteer positions has grown unwieldy. As it is with most nonprofits, there are staff members on board with a high degree of variation in their experience with business software. Training for these users and ease of use are important to make sure any system is accepted by the staff.

Their particular Critical Business Issues were narrowed into a few bullet points after just a few conversations with them and they looked like this:

- ☑ Need for more current and reliable technology
    - ☑ Leverage advances in new technology
    - ☑ Current system used for over 10 years
    - ☑ Need a system that can manage and enable remote employees effectively
- ☑ Want a long-term vendor/partner
    - ☑ Current system has served the organization well

- ☑ It is important that next generation of business systems meet/exceed this experience
- ☑ Ease of use
  - ☑ Staff at multiple locations with varying degrees of business software experience and skills
  - ☑ Ensure the ability to maximize organization resources through improved productivity
- ☑ Revamp of procurement process
  - ☑ Eliminate manual expense management functions while being able to proactively monitor budgets
  - ☑ Current systems require arduous spreadsheet workarounds
- ☑ Reporting updates
  - ☑ Improve the efficiency in creating and distributing critical financial reports to key stakeholders
  - ☑ Funders requiring specific program-relating reporting that not currently able to collect without tedious manual processes
- ☑ Payroll
  - ☑ Need to streamline the organization's personnel management functions while improving the efficiency of the payroll process
  - ☑ Easily manage the seasonality of the employment
- ☑ Data integration
  - ☑ Easier, more efficient import/exports with existing solution (e.g., donor management software, time clock vendor, HR solution, and funder reporting system requirements)

There wasn't anything magical or special about pulling these specific pain points from the organization's collective consciousness. Easily 95% of nonprofits I talk to do not have these types of CBIs written out in a logical format when I am first in contact with them. It is all there though. These issues are the instinctive reasons as to why they believe they need something new to fix all of their ills. They know they have problems and believe a new system will fix what ails them. These issues arise from the volume of staff gripes and complaints about their system felt in everyday business processes.

They may come from funders who are getting late or incomplete reports from your organizations.

A common issue which occurs when organizations start to detail their pain points is not being able to see the forest for the trees. Instead of writing out their overall symptoms they will begin by detailing the surgical steps needed to fix the problem, in other words, outlining the specific features or functionality that individual folks use on a daily basis. The details are important of course, but you have to start at the high level just like you did in your mission statement process. If you can't list out these items correctly then you won't be able to start to prioritize the lower items according to their real importance versus the importance of the one staff member who gripes the most.

Each specific feature and functionality point you eventually ask for needs to reference a CBI and then be ranked in order of importance or need for the organization. Doing so will keep your organization and, more importantly, your potential vendors, focused on your true needs. Vendors won't be able to turn the story to areas they feel they have a particular strength in while ignoring other areas. You will also be giving your potential vendors the flexibility to show their product for what it can help you to do better than what you have today while keeping them focused on the main areas of your concern.

To place this in an easy order, defining your CBIs follows these three steps:

- ☑ **Catalog** - Catalog the various pains felt throughout your organization in relation to the business processes you are hoping to fix. Be exhaustive in writing these out, but ask your staff to not get bogged down in individual functionality annoyances.

- ☑ **Categorize** - Organize the pains into overall categories of discontent. Narrow these categories to just a few main ones. Too many categories make the whole process too complex to manage as we go forward in our buying process. There is beauty in being able to communicate your CBIs in a succinct manner. By being succinct you can avoid the "lost in translation" moments with vendors later on.

- ☑ **Prioritize** - Make sure that each category has a priority to it that helps your staff decide which features are ok to potentially negotiate away and which ones are so important you would rule out a vendor for. I suggest prioritization on every level of planning you do all the way down to specific features and functionalities as you get to that level of detail. Whether you decide to share these priority levels with your potential vendors or not has pros and cons. The pros are to make sure vendors focus on the core issues while the cons include that they will then only focus on those issues and miss showing the big picture and ignore the lower priority items. I recommend you not show the priorities for the CBIs as those should be non-negotiable, but that you do show potential vendors the priority level of specific functionality categories.

I tell prospects all the time the biggest cause of issues between a potential or actual vendor and a prospect or client is mismatched expectations. Bad feelings, lost sales opportunities, or client dissatisfaction with an implementation process are almost always due to poor communication and mismatched expectations. If you can provide your CBIs to a vendor as a roadmap then you will constantly have something to point back to as the line down the middle of the straight road to pull everyone back on track should the process start to wander. If the vendor begins to pressure you to close the sale and you know they haven't satisfied a specific CBI then it becomes an easy conversation to have with the vendor about their mismatched expectation at that point!

At the most basic level a CBI comes down to the fact there isn't a reason to buy anything if there is not a specific pain that makes the purchasing process and the purchase itself worth the effort and the dollars. As you define your Critical Business Issues, be honest with yourself as to what they are since you and your staff will do no one any favors in this process by not dealing in reality. Taking control of your buying process is incumbent on you knowing yourself well enough to communicate your needs to the outer world. If you cannot do that effectively then perhaps you are in a position where, before you do anything, an outside consultant may be the right first step. Think of that as going to premarital counseling as part of our Vendor Dance!

In general though, I don't believe the vast majority of nonprofits need a big consulting contract to figure this all out. You know it instinctively. It's a matter of putting the effort in upfront in a directed manner. It's a matter of getting all of the relevant stakeholders at your organization to understand how doing this part will make the rest of the buying process that much more in your control and easier for all involved. I know you can do this!

Point Two: Organization Outline

Now that your CBIs are defined it will be necessary for you to provide a quick description of your organization to potential vendors. We are creating a new type of organizational profile than you probably have done before. This is your Buyer's Profile. This information is sort of your dating profile within our Vendor Dance. Listing out all of your stats, figures, and items that will help your potential suitors get to know you better will save you both from the pain of multiple dates with a vendor that clearly has no potential or desire for commitment.

The types of things helpful to include in your buying profile for your organization vary greatly. Many vary based upon the type of organization you are and the type of application you are looking to purchase. Some are very standard. These outlines are your first date impressions, so to speak. You, like many nonprofits, have probably spent countless hours on how to present yourself in the best and most complete manner to potential funders, big donors, or on information sources like Guidestar.org or Greatnonprofits.org, but spend almost zero time collecting relevant data when it comes to talking to a potentially mission-critical application vendor for the first time. This relationship will be amazingly important to your mission over time so this type of prep work is as important as the work you do for other introductions. Think of these in the vein of the who, what, when, where, and why questions you learned back in school. Your CBIs are the "Why" in this model.

These include:

- ☑ Definition of your organization's mission
    - ☑ This is your "what," meaning what is this purchase supposed to support
- ☑ An outline of the programs that your mission supports, where that support is offered (local, regional, international)
    - ☑ This is your "who," meaning who is this purchase going to help
- ☑ Key measurable statistics that you measure the success of your mission by
    - ☑ "How" do you measure the success of individual programs of your organization?
    - ☑ "Where" do your CBIs match to each of the various programs?
- ☑ The users of all sorts who might need access to the system you are researching
- ☑ Number of remote offices you have currently to support your mission
    - ☑ List out the various locations where your mission is delivered
- ☑ The information technology infrastructure of your organization and number of IT employees
    - ☑ Important to catalog this data, but, as previously mentioned, don't make it one of the first criteria that will eliminate a solution
- ☑ Any internal Subject Matter Experts you may have on staff

These are just a few of the main items that are good to compile for your "dating profile" about your organization. You may have numerous other factors about your organization that make you unique in your own mission that would be relevant to learn here. You can go as in-depth as you may want. This is also a good place to introduce some of the process mapping we've discussed. It's great to show the vendor you are an organization that understands itself from a process standpoint. Think of what those other items are and add them to the list.

These "Nice-to-knows" may include:

- ☑ Some of the unique history of your organization.
- ☑ Highlights of your mission in the last year.
- ☑ Your last annual report and 990 to send to them. They will look it up anyway. Get ahead of them on the curve. You're selling them a little here by saying what a good potential sale you could be for them. You want to tease them a little bit. To extend our dating analogy, this would be the flirting stage.
- ☑ Any business process mapping that has been done.
- ☑ Sources of your funding
    - ☑ Percentages of funding that is from grants, donations, or other such sources.
- ☑ Specific reporting or communication requirements data regarding those types of issues you are looking to specifically fix. A couple of examples:
    - ☑ If the issue is financial reporting, include information on your chart of accounts and reporting needs for various stakeholders available.
    - ☑ If the issue is fundraising support, detail the type of data you wish to capture on donors and how you would like to use that information internally.
    - ☑ If the issue is volunteer management, share stats on how you need to track the volunteers all the way from time tracking to accounting.
- ☑ And so on....

I could go on and on here. You see the idea though I think.

Point Three: Return on Mission

Return on Mission (ROM) is the ability to look beyond the standard Return on Investment (ROI) formula in order to make sure your investments have the maximum impact on not just the bottom line, but to the maximum impact on the mission itself.

Funders love new projects. Who doesn't like a shiny new car? The ability to get the fantastic photo op of your big winners circle check there with a number of thankful young children sitting around their new computer lab or with their new stack of school supplies is heart-tugging and wonderful. The same photo opportunity value can't be said for the update or fixes to that computer lab the next year. New projects are exciting. Updates or ongoing maintenance? Not so much.

There are so many more grants out there to fund the programs of your nonprofit than there are to fund ongoing infrastructure costs. You will find a few that could technically be called infrastructure because they fund a program's staffing concerns, etc., but as soon as the grant goes away so do the dollars for that infrastructure and the reporting on those resources related to the grant can be amazing. I have seen it change somewhat with a growing understanding among some funders of the need to support infrastructure, but for most you only have a couple of options for your nonprofit when it comes to funding infrastructure: fundraise or be frugal. Nonprofits usually seem to choose all of the above in the answer to that question. Unfortunately, that is an avenue that causes the infrastructure of a nonprofit to suffer.

Software purchases are almost always considered infrastructure items. The license costs of a software purchase represent a big, one-time hit to the bottom line for most nonprofits. Those hits can be hard to deal with and thus are sometimes put off for as long as possible. It is also one main reason, when purchasing, so many organizations just like yours end up purchasing software that is not what they need, but is what they feel they can afford. Never mind all of the extra issues that go into buying software that is not the right fit for your organization for all of the reasons we've already discussed (updates, fixes, workarounds, spreadsheet creep, staff morale, and more).

My first wish in this cycle is that we could change the game so that funders realize the value towards the mission of infrastructure purchases. If more funders would make available grants for strictly infrastructure usage it would be a big game changer. While there are a few out there who will fund infrastructure grants, the vast majority is standard program-based. I believe software purchases, if done correctly for the organization, have a huge return on the mission for the organization.

My second wish here is that we could find a way to make pricing for nonprofits looking to purchase software more transparent. I do not hold out much hope for this anytime soon in that pricing is, as we have discussed, a sales tactic at many vendors. Even a reputable vendor may have a wildly varied price for you at one end of the buying process than at the other end as they change what they want to sell you based upon what they learn about you throughout the process. Pricing is never going to be easy. The best a nonprofit can do is lay out a specific scenario for purchase early on to the vendor not only based upon the number of users needed but also based upon the CBIs already internally identified. Tell the vendor you would expect the price could go 30% or so higher or lower later on as the discussions continue, but that you expect the best effort possible based upon their experience with your set of business issues, type of organization, specific mission, and number of users. From there you can start to have an honest price discussion that begins to look at that price, the functionality they believe you need that you may not have considered, and what the potential "Return on Mission" could look like for you.

I like thinking in terms of "Return on Mission" as it makes the vendor understand what they are providing is not just an investment the organization is making, but it is an investment that should forward the mission of the organization in tangible ways. Every accounting package, website software, donor management package, grants management tool, etc. can and should be sold to you in a way that makes the impact on your mission clear. If the vendor cannot make that case for you then you might want to restate what you are looking for or find another vendor.

Selling to for-profit businesses, be it large or small, is generally a simple study on features, functionality, and, most importantly, return on investment. An example: the software from Company X has these features on our checklist and the software from Company Y only has these features. Company X software is five times more expensive than the software from Company Y. What features and functionality of the software from Company X can we live without in order to save the money or will the extra features provide a greater benefit that ultimately outweighs the cost? Thus, begins the tradeoff game. Sounds familiar doesn't it?

Return on investment (ROI) helps to eliminate the tradeoff game by creating a simple performance measure. Many business people sitting on your boards want to make sure that decisions you make with the donors' dollars are made with this kind of ROI analysis done to it. ROI has been a great tool for BUSINESSES (emphasis added on purpose here to note later point). The ROI measurement is used in business to evaluate the efficiency of an investment or to compare the efficiency of a number of different investments. ROI is a very popular metric because of its versatility and, frankly, its simplicity. That is, if an investment does not have a positive ROI, or if there are other opportunities with a higher ROI, then the equation states that the investment should be not be undertaken or the investment providing the higher ROI should be selected.

Seems fairly straightforward doesn't it? One could only hope it is that easy. So many factors do begin to weave their way into the original formula, but we will stick with the basics here.

Here is the standard ROI formula:

To calculate ROI, the benefit (return) of an investment is divided by the cost of the investment; the result is expressed as a percentage or a ratio.

$$ROI = \frac{(\text{Gain from Investment} - \text{Cost of Investment})}{\text{Cost of Investment}}$$

A quick and easy ROI analysis example for a store:

Assume:
- "Regular" customers visit twice per month
- Average revenue of each visit is $20
- Cost of premium (offer) is $7
- Cost per mailer is $1.08

If 200 offers are mailed each month:
- 10% redeemed = 20 new customers
- 14% become "regulars" = 3 regular customers

Then:
- 3 regular customers spending $40 per month every month for 12 months would bring in an additional annual revenue of $1,440.
- 3 customers x $40 x 12 months = $1,440
- The initial investment of $356 ($216 for advertising and $140 for the giveaway) produced a return of $1,440.
- Return on Investment = 404%

The ROI number can be very subjective in many ways and your vendor may send you a spreadsheet they use to calculate ROI from their point of view. "Gain from Investment" can include hard to measure statistics such as productivity gains, process improvements tied back to employee time savings and the like. ROI, even with its subjective possibilities, is used to try to put realistic investment measurements towards a business decision-making process. As great as that sounds, it is always more complicated when the human element becomes involved.

With **Return on Mission** (ROM) we are working to calculate much as a standard ROI is calculated, but with the extra component of understanding the impact of the purchase on the mission of the organization. I've represented this in the formula below (not necessarily scientific, but helpful to realize that any ROI must make a positive impact to a piece of mission criteria):

$$\text{ROM} = \frac{(\text{Gain from Investment} - \text{Cost of Investment}) / \text{Cost of Investment}}{\text{Impact to Mission}}$$

The **"Impact to Mission"** is to be based upon the particular mission of your organization, of course. If you serve meals to the homeless, for example, then every purchase made should be seen not just for the productivity gains it could give your organization's employees, but in the light of how it can help your organization serve more meals, advocate for your cause, or purchase more supplies.

As a nonprofit executive what are you told over and over again by board members, consultants, and your resident helpful "know-it-alls"? They say, in the nicest of intentions of course, "You need to act more like a business." The implication being that, as a nonprofit, there is little resemblance to being a real business. They miss the fact that, just like any other work out there, a nonprofit relies on marketing, sound accounting, a core vision and principles, human resources, rent, and so much more. The only difference is in outcome. The corporation lives to make a profit whereas the nonprofit, many would seem to think, lives solely to not make a profit. They don't realize a nonprofit can make a profit. The money just has to be, at the end of the day, given towards the philanthropic mission instead of, for example, as dividends to shareholders. Thus, the importance of **Return on Mission**.

> ### A quick and easy ROM analysis example for a new large printer/copier solution:
>
> **Assume:**
> - Print 10,000 pages per month on current printer/copier
> - Current printer/copier costs $0.02 per printed page
> - New printer/copier costs $800.00
>
> **If new printer/copier costs $0.01 per printed page:**
> - New copier/printer has half the cost per printed page
> - Monthly printing costs from $200 to $100.
> - Gain $200.00 in trade-in on old printer/copier
>
> **Then:**
> - ($100 printing savings per month x 12) - ($1000 for new copier/printer - $200 for trade-in) = $400 savings over 1 year
> - The initial investment of $600 ($800 for the new printer/copier minus the $200 trade-in for the older printer/copier) produced a return of $400 in the first year of production.
> - Standard Return on Investment = 33%
>
> **Return On Mission Calculation for this scenario:**
> - $400 savings in first year of production / $400 (a sample amount of one month of electricity cost at a children's shelter building) = 100% return on identified mission costs.

The goal of an exercise like this is to make tangible the reality of a new business application purchase to all of the stakeholders at your organization and for the vendor to always keep in mind that every decision is rationalized and justified by how it affects the mission of the organization.

As you map your CBIs back to your mission and the vendor maps its functionality points back to your CBIs, the Return on Mission gives all involved a tangible understanding of how all those pieces will all come together to serve the organization best.

Point Four: Doable Logistics

I am going to spend a little extra time here than you might think and I will do that for the sheer fact that being organized in your buying process is a big key to being in control of it.

"Doable logistics" refers to the pieces of the process you can nail down as milestones for your discussion with your vendors. The term "logistics" may not be comfortable for some people, but all I am referring to is the ability to set guidelines to manage your communications most effectively. The pieces that definitely should be included within these guidelines are items such as timeframe, your potential budget, communications' process and demonstration schedule. There are other factors that are different for every organization, but these few are the basics that should absolutely be covered. Other than these basics you need to make sure you have your milestones set out and agreed upon prior to your real contact with potential vendors. The reason this is important to you is these milestones are one manner in which potential vendors will judge you as a prospect during your initial Vendor Dance conversations. Your ability to articulate these to them will absolutely determine what type of treatment and attention you will receive from them. That isn't necessarily right, but it is how things work and you want to have these impressions tilt to your advantage as best as possible at all times.

Let's walk through a few of these now.

Timeframe

Most folks think of "buying timeframe" as only the date when the organization wishes to make a decision as to which particular business application software they would like to finally buy. While that is certainly a deadline which needs to be understood by everyone involved, the more pressing date is the day you would like your bright, shiny new application to be live and in production (aka useful and working) in your office. As a sales rep gauging a nonprofit buying cycle we are taught to walk dates backwards from that date to then help a potential customer understand by when they need to make a purchasing decision in order to have enough time for a proper application implementation process. Side bar here in that this is one more reason I don't like RFPs. They put arbitrary purchase dates out there with generally unreasonable implementation schedules for the type of project being undertaken. The nonprofits and consultants decide when they can, according to their budget and schedule, buy, as opposed to making a purchase decision with a solid understanding of the length of time and complexity of implementing what they are looking to buy.

Let's try an example of walking backwards to find our desired decision timeframe. If you are planning a walk/run event for October 1st then your true decision timeframe for purchase of software to help manage and run the event would need to be based upon a walk back from the date you need the software to be live in order for you to begin to use it for your event planning.

October 1st   **Your Walk/Run Event**

July 15th   **Registration and fundraising begins.**

The fun begins!

Apr 15th   **Database/Registration system live for staff**

I've seen organizations typically have a preference of about forty-five days before registration starts. This makes time for database organization, web/communication tools' final tweaks, staff training and readiness, and all of the other myriad tasks that go into getting a walk/run event on its way to success.

March 1st   **Purchase date for software.**

How did we find this date? Based on polling our vendors for this particular type of software we found that six weeks from purchase is a safe and acceptable amount of time needed for the implementation tasks to be accomplished with the least amount of drama. Assuming that we need to allow for six weeks of implementation, testing, data conversion/import, training, and other tasks, this date makes for a good target date. Also remember the vendor you are talking to may not be available to start the day after you sign the contract. Especially at larger organizations there could be several business days from the time your contract is signed and the time you are assigned some type of implementation specialist. It may then be several more business days before the first implementation team discussions are finalized. Be sure to understand clearly your specific vendor's process transition from the sales team to the implementation team. Get an understanding of how many business days there are from contract to implementation team first discussions. This is an easy spot to have mismatched expectations.

Many nonprofits like to, towards the end of a sales process, ask who will be leading their implementation. You probably won't get the answer you were hoping for or be able to ask for a particular implementation services team member because of scheduling conflicts so it is worth knowing the types of people who may be implementing your project, but you won't know the specific person assigned to your project until you sign on the dotted line and the sale is closed. Those implementation resources are always, except for the biggest customers out there, doled out on a first-come-first-served basis. Once you do sign your contract you are, understandably, probably very excited about getting moving on your new project. To then slam the brakes on your excitement because your vendor's implementation team won't be available for more than a phone call or some emails for a couple of weeks is not fun. Ask the tough questions at the end of your sales process to understand how you will be transitioned from the sales process to the implementation process. If you can't get good answers here that is a definite red flag.

If you feel that you are going to be tight on your implementation timeframe you probably want to adjust your purchasing schedule ahead rather than try to squeeze the implementation team on the back end where mistakes or omissions could make life very difficult as you work to go live on your new application.

January 1st   **Contact vendors for information and begin sales process.**

A basic sales cycle could be completed in sixty days. If that sounds long to you I can understand, but remember the chapter where I outlined how many meetings can go into this process? Trying to squeeze something like that into forty-five to sixty days is extremely challenging. It can be shorter if you have the vendor basics out of the way and are ready to roll, but I would encourage you, that even if you are going to purchase from a vendor you have purchased from before, remember each new sales cycle is a chance for a level set of your relationship together. Like a couple celebrating an anniversary who take the time to discuss their relationship, those are great times to make sure your expectations still line up together. Most sales cycles are ninety days or longer. I sometimes talk about sales cycles with nonprofits being two 90-day processes. These two 90-day processes are not necessarily sequential either. The first set of ninety days could be the research phase to get budgetary estimates put into the next year's fiscal plan and identify potential vendors. The second set of ninety days would be the actual stretch run to an actual purchase. I've had these two-step, 90-day sales cycles be a year apart before. Patience is required, but so also is the appropriate amount of urgency.

3 - 6 months' prior   **Search for and review various vendors.**

Here is what I would refer to as that first 90-day cycle as described above. This is the time when you are gathering information about the various options out there and what could work for you. Checking with your peers on what has worked for them, gathering marketing information, going to a seminar or tradeshow, and all of those other types of activities are at work here.

    Walking backwards is an extremely effective way to have a clear vision for where you need to establish your purchase decision date. Understanding what is involved for the implementation of the system you are purchasing is incredibly important to make your walk back realistic. Your potential vendor should be able to, just as we discussed with regard to pricing, relay to you what a customer of your general circumstances could expect for an implementation timeframe. Most likely they can even tell you what resources will be necessary from your organization to help the process move along a little faster.

A system, as described above, may only need a few weeks to put together all of the website, database, and communications tools necessary to get started. A new accounting system, for example, could take six months to a year to be ready to go live for your office. Each type of application, based on its complexity, will require a timeframe for implementation that your vendor should be able to help you with based upon their experience with other nonprofits like yourselves implementing in similar environments. No vendor is going to be excited about trying to estimate an implementation timeframe for you without first completing the standard due diligence they require for such an estimation. You will hear every caveat known to humankind tossed at you as qualifiers to any timeframe they will give you. That's ok. Those caveats are helpful to you to understand some of the pitfalls in the implementation process the vendor might expect. This knowledge also tells you what information they are going to want from you prior to getting the final estimate you will need for your decision. Take it all into account. All information flow is a positive. Capture all of the information you can and keep going.

Defining Your Potential Budget

Over the years, vendors have put a lot of thought, time, and energy, all of which not necessarily productive, into trying to decide which organizations will be quality, potential buyers of their products without the benefit of having an organization tell them what their potential budget is for an application purchase. Many graphs and charts are used to help sales reps decide if a particular type of organization will likely have the budget to afford the application they sell. You will be judged by your budget size, types of funding sources, particular mission, number of employees, number of field offices, types of events you manage, and many more criteria too numerous and dizzying to mention here. The chances are if you are getting a marketing piece in the mail or in your email you have been selected by those companies as targets because the vendor believes you may have a chance at affording their software.

A vendor has decided you may be in their target market for their software. That doesn't mean you can afford it. I'm not going to try to tell you how to go through the creation of your own budgeting process here and decide what should or should not be the high/low numbers you target for your potential project budget, but I am going to talk about how to get pricing information from your potential vendors in order to help set realistic expectations for your staff as to what certain levels of software functionality cost.

I will tell you it doesn't work to go into your buying process with specific numbers in mind and then start to knock out certain vendors based on price right out of the box. Remember the CBI discussion. You are buying based upon your needs first. Yes, your eyes may be bigger than your budget when you see things you really like, but could never afford. That becomes a waste of your time and the vendors. That begs the questions: How do you budget for an application when you have no idea how much it costs? If I don't how much it costs how do I budget anything or know I'm talking to the right company? The tough answer is you really don't know until you make a few calls to vendors and start asking those pricing questions we discussed.

Another good means of information are others you may know who have purchased from companies you are looking at. As I mentioned, I would love to see pricing be more transparent for the nonprofit marketplace. Maybe someday we will get there. Until then you'll have to utilize the strategies I discussed for finding pricing based upon your CBIs. If all of the pricing you receive comes back as too high for your taste then looking at the prioritization of those needs may be in order. See which ones you could possibly pull out into separate projects and whether or not that will help bring the cost down. It is usually fairly simple for vendors to pull out some functionality that may add the cost of another software module and lower your estimate. It's worth checking into. You may have to go through an iterative process in order to find applications that fit your needs and your potential budget.

You may also decide to try to go for more budget appropriation to get what you need in full. Many a CFO has called me to ask about costing scenarios only to tell me, "Well, I've put X amount of dollars in our budget as a placeholder." I know off the bat there could be a mismatched expectation of what my product will cost them or the call to me is barking up the wrong application tree. There are quite a few vendors out there who will not want to send you any kind of a price list or even profess to have one. Trust me. Somewhere, somehow they do. They may not be excited to show it to you because giving you a price is part of a strategic sales step for them, but it is there.

Communication Process During the Sale

Maintaining control of the buying process means also maintaining control of all communications with the vendor during the sales process. Vendors need to know who their main point of contact is and who will be available for discussions and when. Each contact at an organization becomes a potential source for information for the vendor. Sales reps will try to develop their internal coaches or champions who will tell them the off-the-record scoop that will help them beat their competition. If all of your vendors are there trying to develop their own champions and gaining advantage via leaked conversation and details then you have already lost control no matter how well you think you are managing the formal communications. All too often an organization will go to the extreme by shutting off all communications to a vendor by creating -- what sales reps call -- gatekeepers. These gatekeepers will try to keep all communications going through them. This stifles available knowledge and information that could be important to the organization in their buying process. The middle ground is to allow communications with the vendor, but let all employees and vendors know that their communications are to be reported and catalogued. If you then find out anyone has violated that policy you will have an untrustworthy vendor on your hands and a difficult employee to deal with. Communication is a good thing. It should be encouraged. Just avoid, as we've heard around Washington, DC, so often, the appearance of impropriety. If all communications are kept above board then the vendors will not be able to use back channel discussions as a way to influence potential decision makers. Champions of a particular product or two should be encouraged within an organization. These champions within an organization are often scared to speak up because the "boss" doesn't allow for it or they worry sharing their opinion would disqualify them from being involved in the decision. Quite the opposite should happen. Champions should be required and enjoy the opportunity to sell the points of their favorite products in a safe internal environment outside of the influence of the vendors' salespeople. I've seen those debates be extremely healthy for organizations.

Demonstration Schedule

At some point you will, of course, want to see a demonstration of the products you are taking into consideration. I would be quite surprised if you decided you could buy a product without seeing it first. It would be like buying a car without test driving it. It can be done, but you had better know the person you are buying from or the exact type of car extremely well. There are some good ways and some bad ways to drive these presentations for your vendors.

I'm not as concerned with the venue of the demos as I am with the content and presentation of these demonstrations. Vendors will offer you the opportunity to view demonstrations of their products via the multitude of online tools as well as in-person demonstrations. What type of demonstration will be offered for you will honestly depend upon the type and expense of the product you are reviewing.

Simple economics of the expense of people traveling across the country to a meeting dictate the sale should be commensurate to the expenses involved in the sales process. Two plane tickets, a couple of hotel rooms, and other travel expenses can easily add up to over a couple of thousand dollars. Those are expenses that solutions from vendors of lower-priced products cannot afford. The flip side to the need for that expense is the more expensive the solution, the more complicated the solution is, the more necessary it is to take the time to view a large-scale, in-person demonstration of the product. I am discussing a product demonstration in terms of the economics for the vendor in order for you to be able to set the proper expectations for what type of sales demonstrations and attention you will receive from a vendor.

Vendors are constantly reviewing their "Cost of Sales" against the actual profit from a sale in the same way you look at programs versus expense line items. As a sales rep I have been trained to think of the sales I make as paying for my job plus five to ten other jobs at the company. If I don't make the sales necessary it isn't just my job on the line, but others throughout the company who I may not even know. No pressure, right? I've worked at smaller companies most of my career so I have seen the direct result of a lack of sales from a rep, otherwise known as a high cost of sales, and I've seen friends of mine laid off. It is easier to hide the personal effects of a lack of sales at a bigger company where there are more people to be a buffer for the bad reps. My point is companies always take sending out resources seriously. Being respectful of the sales team resources will go a long way towards gaining the respect of the team of your potential vendors. If they see you want to understand how they can sell to you based upon the type of application you are looking to buy from them then you are setting yourself up for a positive relationship after the sale with the vendor you ultimately choose.

No matter the actual venue of your demonstrations (webinar, personal webinar, or in-house personal demo) it is important you see two types of demonstrations: the overview and the personalized. The overview demo you should see is the corporate-speak demo that is scripted, canned and ready to go to show their product highlights as the vendor sees them. It's a little like watching a late night infomercial, but worth seeing because you will learn what the vendor believes they do best. Take copious notes on the overview demo for two reasons: (1) To be able to see what the vendor sees as the Critical Business Issues their software solves out of the box (match that against your already created CBIs to see if there is a decent match), and (2) to make sure that nothing major changes between what you see on the overview demo and your eventual personalized demo. It happens sometimes. Remember the Russian phrase, "Trust, but verify"?

For the personalized demo you need to take control of the script. Too many times the nonprofit will try to lay out specific feature sets they wish to present in a demo. A demo then becomes a laundry list of boring feature checklists. Eyes of all involved glass over when the lights go out and the vendor does what we call "show up and throw up" of all their best features. I know that sounds gross, but it refers to when I, or another sales rep, shows up with our technical sales engineer and proceed to talk non-stop for three hours without interruption. Nothing could be worse for you, the potential client, or more boring and dissatisfying for the vendor. My job in a demo situation, when the technical sales engineer is leading the showcase of the application, is to try to elicit responses from the customer's staff and get a real conversation going. To that end, your best personalized demo involves you working on an agenda with the vendor that will involve the following:

- ☑ **Demo to your CBIs** - Demo the product from the point of view of your unique CBIs. Have your organization's CBIs listed somewhere all can see and make sure the vendors know to explain how their solution will solve those CBIs. If they can't remember to do that after being told to do so then it is a red flag for you. It will make you wonder if they are just not doing a competent job in their demo or in their preparation for it or maybe they don't feel they can solve your CBIs, not want to admit it, and are attempting to showcase something else they do instead.

- ☑ **Demo to your processes** - Make sure they understand how their functionality will fit into the processes you have identified as needing fixing. If they describe a new way of revamping a process you have jointly discussed ensures the end result is the same or better than identified. Make sure you gather data on the mapping points inside the process as they've described it and see if there is a verifiable way to judge their claims (reference, whitepaper, etc.).

- ☑ **Demo to unique points of the product** - This should not be hard. Every vendor wants to show you their whiz bang stuff. Make sure you give them the opportunity to do so somehow during their demo. If none of their whiz bang pieces match to your CBIs or processes right now still pack in a few minutes of time in the demo for them to showcase something special for you. You will probably learn something and you will definitely get an idea of the vision the company has regarding the future of its products. Hopefully that future will relate to your needs down the line and you will have a vendor you can have a long-term relationship with.

Following these points will ensure you gather the information necessary within your demos to make the decisions you need to make. It will also guarantee you do not get led down paths during these demos that will tell you a lot of great information but not help you understand how to solve your problems. After all, that is the point of the demonstrations. I can't begin to tell you how many sales I have won for the sheer fact I followed those rules above and my competition did not.

Extras Good to Know

These are little lists of the items I have liked or disliked that a nonprofit has done during a sales process:

- ☑ **Travel suggestions** - If out of town travel is involved, it is wonderful to have help with hotel and travel suggestions for the area. Always nice to get a quality recommendation for a decent hotel in a city I may not know well.

- ☑ **Meeting space logistics** - It is just plain nice when the prospect has the logistics for a meeting down, i.e., a meeting room that matches comfortably the number of people invited, easy internet access instructions, a decent projector, a screen or the right-sized wall, and even something as simple as help to find the restroom.

- ☑ **Focus on us while we're there** ("Focus Power," as the saying from *The Karate Kid* goes) - Ask staff to leave the smartphone or other such devices alone except for note-taking only. It's amazingly distracting to see people constantly checking their Blackberry for their email as we are trying to demo to a specific detailed point.

- ☑ **Help us keep your staff on schedule** - Manage break times and remember I want to catch a plane on time and get home just as much as other attendees would like to get home or back to work on time, too. Break times during a demo are pure escape for a lot of folks. Five minutes becomes ten, and ten-minute breaks become fifteen minutes. Keeping people on task and coming back from breaks is important for the vendor to keep the flow going correctly and for the nonprofit to make sure that all of the points are understood in a cohesive fashion. I've often wanted to co-opt the video from the beginning of a movie which asks the moviegoers to turn off all cell phones or not text during the movie. We do it for movies; surely we can do it for a presentation for something that is this important. Just a small pet peeve. Can you tell?

- ☑ **Brevity in proposal responses** - Tell vendors to leave out sales brochures or other materials in their proposal responses. Demand short and to the point responses. Brevity may be the soul of wit, but it is also the key to understanding. Too many words leave room for many doubts and cover-ups. At Kintera we had a Word template that would automatically insert the right marketing language depending upon the proposal being created. It was a monstrosity at times with fifty to sixty pages of what was actually good information, but the customers would just look at the table of contents and go straight to the pricing first. Tell the vendors what you want and expect out of a proposal response to keep everything on the level.

- ☑ **Competitor situation** – Oftentimes, a potential customer likes to keep a secret regarding who they are reviewing in their buying process. I have never understood that. It's a pretty small world at times in the vendor community and many of us know each other from selling against each other for years and years. The customers who are open as to who the main competitors of the deal are get more benefit out of it than those who try to keep such secret. All vendors will want to know who they are up against and have created strategic competitive battle cards for their main opponents that detail the strengths and weaknesses of their products in relation to their own. It is unseemly to have a sales rep talk down or truly ill of another company or product. Those who will really go the negative politics route are reps or vendors I would shy away from personally as that will give a hint as to their personality later on in your relationship with them. The ones who will share with you the good and bad, as they see it, about another vendor in an open and honest discussion will be very helpful to you in your discussions. It will also give you a hint as to their willingness to be open and honest about future problems that may come down the road. So don't be afraid to tell each vendor who the competition is and ask them for a frank discussion about how they feel they compete and win as well as lose against each of those vendors.

Wrapping it up

The Nonprofit Buyer Model of Control, if followed, will put you in control of your buying processes in a way you have never before been able to do. It will remove the mystery from these situations, save everyone a good deal of time and effort, and produce a final outcome – the actual purchase – more in line with the needs of the organization. A relationship that starts off on the right foot will, more often than not, lead to a long-term relationship built on trust and understanding. The end of the Vendor Dance is the actual marriage between the now customer and the vendor. What the Nonprofit Buyer Model of Control has brought together let no one put asunder.

Chapter summary:

Your Nonprofit Buyer Model of Control is a means to have a new kind of buying relationship with your vendors. It consists of these four main points:

- ☑ **CBIs** - The definition of your very own Critical Business Issues, the high level reasons your organization needs to make this particular purchase.

- ☑ **Organization Outline** - The definition of your organization's mission, users of all sorts who might need access to the system you are researching, and the like.

- ☑ **Return on Mission** - Explanations of how you expect your purchase to impact the mission of the organization.

- ☑ **Doable Logistics** - A nice explanation for the vendor as to your timeframe, budget, and communication process during the sale along with other good relationship expectations.

By following the lessons inside these four main points, your organization will be able to balance its relationship with its vendors, match expectations for purchase and eventual delivery, and articulate an accurate Return on Mission for your board, staff, funders, and donors.

Bringing it home:

- ☑ Think of a current, painful business process you have and try to spend ten to fifteen minutes outlining the high level CBIs per the process in this chapter.

- ☑ Could you relate that process to an impact on your mission in order to have a Return on Mission quotient?

- ☑ Take that business pain and think about when you would want to have your "fix" installed and perform the walk-back exercise.

- ☑ Look through your organization to understand how you would organize your buying team according to "Doable Logistics."

"Enjoying success requires the ability to adapt. Only by being open to change will you have a true opportunity to get the most from your talent."

                Nolan Ryan
                Hall of Fame Major League Baseball Pitcher

CHAPTER EIGHT

Sales Stage	Percent to Sales Close	Stage Description
1	10%	Why This Matters
2	20%	The Nonprofit Buyer
3	30%	Unreliable Buying Techniques
4	40%	The Other Side of the Fence
5	50%	How a Sales Process Works on You
6	60%	Sales 101
7	70%	The Nonprofit Buyer Model of Control
8	80%	Adapting to your organization
9	90%	Closing the sale
10	100%	Deal done! On to the next one...

What the Nonprofit Buyer Model of Control has just defined for you is, I am sure, what will be quite a cultural shift for you in your own nonprofit organization and its buying processes. All of the old ways of interaction between you and your potential vendors that created artificial boundaries and relationships built on an "us versus them" conflict mentality now can be tossed out. When you are able to enter into a buying process with a potential vendor from a position of control, you will be able to not only purchase what you need for your organization, but you will be in a position to have your potential vendors show you what is possible beyond your imagination.

If you follow the Nonprofit Buyer Model of Control you will also be forcing a cultural shift at your potential vendors as well. For many vendors that cultural shift will be well beyond the effects you may feel inside your own organization. Your vendors, for good or bad, have been setting the table for your purchases and this model will now encourage a more balanced relationship between potential customer and vendor.

The next question that is logical is, "How do I set up my organization to use this model of control?" The answer: Three ways.

- ☑ 1) Communication
- ☑ 2) Planning
- ☑ 3) Discipline

Communication

Developing your CBIs requires your organization to have an honest communication with itself about the pains it is currently feeling and the needs those pains are creating. Getting open and constructive feedback throughout the organization where the specific processes affect job performance is critical to the entire rest of the process. If your organization cannot be honest and real during the creation of the CBIs then the rest of the model is a house of cards because you will be asking vendors to solve problems which either don't exist or aren't that important. You will then end up with a solution at the end destined to fail.

My dire warnings here aren't meant to make you feel like this is a hard thing to do. It really isn't. Your leadership will need to make clear to all the goal of the process and encourage the feedback. However, for that to work in your organization, you will need to encourage positive information gathering. Enable those who are emotionally invested in your mission to give their feedback freely, yet constructively. Don't let it turn into a gripe-fest. Make sure you stay positive. That can be the hard part. Dealing with negative issues is never really a comfortable situation. Uncovering all of the pains and broken processes is, however, the only way to ensure your mission is a success as you move forward so it must be done. Thankfully, you probably have a staff that cares about the mission of your organization and want to be a part of the betterment of it. Rely on that passion and that caring, by letting people know what may feel like busy work actually connects to the mission itself. By communicating openly, positively, staying true to the mission, and focused on real CBIs you will create an atmosphere of cooperation which will lay the foundation for a quality purchasing process.

Planning

The first job in the planning portion of a buying process is to establish the roles of everyone in your organization during the process. Who will be assigned to each vendor for regular communications? Who will be available for technical discussions? Who will need to be involved in the demonstration meetings? Who will play general contractor, as it were, for everyone involved to make sure that the organization's needs are being met at every step in the process? Depending upon your staff these jobs may be done by a small group of employees or it could be a rather large crowd. The main job of your "general contractor" is to keep everyone on task at all points during the process. I do recommend this person be a person of authority or someone with assigned authority in the organization, that everyone is aware of the job, and not necessarily the person who is the ultimate decision maker. It is tough for someone who is that ultimate decision maker to also be that person who is herding all of the cats. The keys to planning success are knowing your role and having a defined general contractor who keeps the ball rolling towards the ultimate goal.

Discipline

This is tough for any and all companies, governmental entities, or nonprofits entering into a business process. In politics they call it "staying on message." It can be tough because people get excited during a process and start to profess loyalties and may engage in communications or subtle messages without even thinking they are doing something that may harm the overall effort being undertaken. If you are in an "us versus them" sales environment or mindset then what I just said sounds like a batten down the hatches approach and limit any and all communication to your vendors. That isn't my point. I mentioned above you may have specific representatives for individual vendors. Those people could be champions for that specific vendor and really want to push that solution. That is great because it will stir the type of debate necessary to uncover the positives and the negatives about that solution. It is possible to have several people working with a particular vendor's sales team and still be able to stay on message and encourage a champion. As long as everyone understands their roles, the ultimate message is maintained, and all involved understand how the decision process is to be carried out, then you can have a variety of interaction with your vendors at several levels and still keep control over the decision process itself. Staying disciplined is important. The undesirable vendor will try to circumvent your control/discipline. The helpful vendor will appreciate your discipline and support.

A balanced relationship with your vendor even after the sale

Once your sale is completed, your balanced relationship with your new vendor will then have the opportunity to continue long after your implementation. One of the best ways that I would encourage you to create deeper bonds with your vendor is through the referral process.

A happy customer who is willing to tell others about their positive experiences with their vendors is the ultimate prize for any vendor. That referral is worth a hundred times what could ever be spent on a marketing campaign. Add to that the turnover in the nonprofit world and I have seen the same person buy from the same vendor two, three, and even 4 times at different organizations. That person will be recruited to solve the ills at another nonprofit after being deemed successful at the one they are at and then proceed to change things up at the new nonprofit by implementing the same slew of applications that worked so well at the other nonprofit. Too bad there is not a one-size-fits-all nonprofit business application suite out there, as these efforts do not necessarily work time and time again when applied equally. It works out well for the vendor though. An easier sales process, little competition, and little to no marketing expense needed to gain the customer. That is a formula for some high software product margin if I've ever seen one.

Sorry if that sounded cynical there. I don't mean to degrade the actual quality relationships that can exist between a vendor and a nonprofit professional, but remember to keep in mind that the sales professional is there to sell something. No matter how well you may get along or trust that person it does not mean that their product is always the right one for your current organization. It is what it is, I'm afraid.

I've seen studies in the past that said that someone happy with a product is only going to tell three or four people about their positive experience whereas that same person with a negative experience will tell eight to ten people. The negative customer reference is obviously one the vendor hopes to avoid, but those three or four good references are golden. You can see how valuable a positive experience and a happy customer are to a company. If you are a happy customer with a company and their work for you I would encourage you to tell that company how happy you are and offer to be of help. The rewards can be numerous. Additional support, input to product feature development, extra passes to user conferences, and speaking engagements are all items you will be offered and could be very good for both your career and nonprofit. You obviously don't want to become a shill for the company in nonprofit clothing, but there are positive things to being supportive when the situation calls for it. As Frank Burns of the TV show *M*A*S*H* once said: "It's nice to be nice to the nice."

Tips for being a good customer referral

- ☑ Be a positive, but realistic referral. Tell the vendor exactly what you would tell a potential customer if they asked you to talk to them. Also tell them why you would say that. You want to be supportive, but you do have professional ethics to account for every day.

- ☑ Respect your own time. Your time is valuable. Set guidelines for how many and what type of calls or visits you will accept over a certain timeframe. Most vendors will try not to have one customer be a reference too often for fear of burnout from the time commitment. You should help manage that expectation as well. Don't feel guilty for saying no, that it isn't a good time. Make sure they know that no doesn't mean you aren't still satisfied, but their application isn't the only thing you do for your job. They will understand.

- ☑ Communicate with your vendor. Be sure to let the vendor know once the potential customer has talked with you and the nature of the conversation. This is a step in the sales process for them and any intelligence on the matter is greatly appreciated.

Hopefully your vendor will have a special way to thank you for providing the positive reference. It's the polite and respectful thing to do for someone.

How to get a positive response in a negative situation

If you are not happy with your vendor I would encourage you to express your frustration, but there are effective ways to make sure they really listen to you.

- ☑ Document everything. If you are having issues with your vendor it is important to have your concerns documented both at the vendor and in your own systems. Once you get elevated to the next set of management to hear your concern there is no guarantee all of your issues will have been effectively documented in their systems.

- ☑ Avoid the nasty letter if at all possible. Many people who are angry about a situation want to send nasty letters outlining their gripes and lack of satisfaction. They will run straight to the CEO if they think it is necessary to get good service. Though it is good to let them know of your issues, many forget they are dealing with real people who are really just trying to do the best they can. I liken it to sending food back at a restaurant. If it has to be done, an understanding and appreciative attitude is more likely to get a positive result than crying foul over bad fowl. Pleading your issues with a hint of understanding at the situation, a willingness to bend within limits, and offers to be supportive once the issues are cleared up will go a long way to having a vendor bend over backwards to help you.

- ☑ Don't let the vendor fall back on procedure. Vendors setup procedures for good reasons usually. They are there to ensure positive support is given to every customer equally. What procedures don't do well at, and why they madden us at times, is account for the extraordinary. Procedures assume all things happen in a logic tree environment. Unfortunately the real world isn't always like that. The vast majority of vendors are not intentionally trying to avoid fixing your problem or being helpful. The procedures can just get in the way of the visibility of your problems.

- ☑ Put your advocates to work on your behalf. During your buying process your sales rep worked hard to find advocates for their product within your organization. Now you can work your relationships at the vendor to your benefit. Contacting your sales rep and asking for his/her help to be your internal advocate is a great way to get visibility for your issues within the vendor. Sales reps can give your issue awareness through different channels other than support and just might be able to be the squeaky wheel you need on your side.

- ☑ Hold back on invoking the contract until absolutely necessary. This is your final straw. Once you start invoking the contract you have essentially a broken relationship with your vendor. Communications and help in the normal give and take are broken down and you are closer than anyone would like to think to actual legal action or mediation. Unless you are really at this point with your vendor do not even casually start to talk about contract clauses. If you are worried about your vendor at all or have special support needs you know about going into your relationship with the vendor then put in structures upfront in the contract to measure against it with biannual or annual review meetings rather than signing a standard contract and waiting till something bad happens to initiate a process.

These are only a few tips to help you prepare your organization for a new type of relationship with your vendors both before and after the sale. You have the opportunity and the skills within your organization today to put this model to work for your mission.

Chapter summary

The logical question after learning the Nonprofit Buyer Model of Control is, "How do I set up my organization to use this model of control?" The answer we discussed comes in the three points of Communication, Planning, and Discipline. In the framework of these points you can align your organization to the model of control and set yourself up for success. Once you have successfully purchased via the model, it will then be time to extend that new type of relationship to being a customer. You and your vendor can work together to help each make your decision more valuable to your organization year after year by continuing to keep the honest lines of communication open and talking about what will help each of you. The balanced relationship between customer and vendor doesn't stop when you sign on the bottom line. If you both work at it then you can both be successful together for years to come. That is when the Vendor Dance goes on from courtship to become a long and successful marriage

Bringing it home

- ☑ How would you set up your organization to use the Nonprofit Buyer Model of Control using the three points of Communication, Planning, and Discipline?

- ☑ Have you ever been a reference, positively or negatively, for a vendor?

- ☑ What were the three or four key points that made you want to be a positive reference for a vendor?

"The buck stops here."
President Harry Truman

CHAPTER NINE

Sales Stage	Percent to Sales Close	Stage Description
1	10%	Why This Matters
2	20%	The Nonprofit Buyer
3	30%	Unreliable Buying Techniques
4	40%	The Other Side of the Fence
5	50%	How a Sales Process Works on You
6	60%	Sales 101
7	70%	The Nonprofit Buyer Model of Control
8	80%	Adapting to your organization
9	90%	Closing the sale
10	100%	Deal done! On to the next one...

There is generally a competitive streak inside every sales rep. I admit that I have one. I do like to win. I do try hard in all that I do. Once, my own father had to sit me out of a soccer game because I wasn't being a good sport out of my desire to win. I've learned to moderate my competitive streak over the years. Golf was a humbling sport for me to learn as it taught me a new level of patience and a new definition of what is a "win." However, there is a rush to "closing the sale." It feels great to bring in the deal. Being able to pull together a solution the team at the new client is excited about is a wonderful feeling. I remember getting the CFO signature on a services contract with a hospital early on in my sales career, circa 1995, and walking through the halls of the hospital wanting to jump up and down like I had just shot a winning soccer goal. Every deal I have ever closed has had a great and satisfying feeling to it.

More so than my own personal satisfaction in closing the deal is the enjoyment I get in seeing an organization excited about their purchase. I get to have a tangible result that what I have done is going to help someone in their work. That always feels good. I can tell when the relationship changes towards the end of the sales process as we move towards signing a deal because the employees of the organization start letting down their guard around me and my team. They start talking more freely and I begin to feel like we are one team. Those are great times when I get to hear the new ideas they have on how to utilize their shiny new toy for their organization. The employees will have taken ownership of the application before the organization has even actually signed the deal to literally own the software. Those are the best times in the process for me because I, for at least a short amount of time, get to feel as if I am a part of your team and a part of your mission.

You are now armed with a powerful toolset to help your organization. By utilizing your newfound understanding of how a sales process works on you, what it is like on the other side of the fence, and the Nonprofit Buyer Model of Control to help you as a buyer, your organization can now be more effective and make the buying process one that is a positive step forward for your organization rather than a painful slog everyone dreads. You will be able to, in your own buying process, learn more about yourselves and about your vendor options than you could have ever previously known.

This new relationship model between nonprofit and vendor will give you the balanced relationship necessary to ensure every need is identified, every pain is solved, every solution proposed and ultimately purchased extends the capabilities for you to fulfill your organization's mission.

And after all, that is what this is all about.

"Without continual growth and progress, such words as improvement, achievement, and success have no meaning."
Benjamin Franklin (1706–1790)
American statesman, scientist, and printer

CHAPTER TEN

Sales Stage	Percent to Sales Close	Stage Description
1	10%	Why This Matters
2	20%	The Nonprofit Buyer
3	30%	Unreliable Buying Techniques
4	40%	The Other Side of the Fence
5	50%	How a Sales Process Works on You
6	60%	Sales 101
7	70%	The Nonprofit Buyer Model of Control
8	80%	Adapting to your organization
9	90%	Closing the sale
10	100%	Deal done! On to the next one...

The hard work now done, I thought it would be great to step back and have a little fun. In this chapter we will wander through some basic sales acronyms and a typical sales compensation plan. Maybe not your typical idea of fun, but I think you'll enjoy it. As with any job, there is a vocabulary of shared common experience. The goal of this chapter is to give you a little look into the vocabulary of sales and what the compensation plans can look like for your hard-working sales types out there. I think you'll find this info interesting and, hopefully, a little fun to learn!

Know Your Jargon otherwise known as "Death by TLAs"

"History and origins. The exact term *three-letter acronyms* appeared in the literature in 1975...They are used in many other fields, but the term TLA is particularly associated with computing... In 1988, eminent computer scientist Edsger W Dijkstra wrote 'Because no endeavour is respectable these days without a TLA ...By 1992 it was in a Microsoft handbook. Use of 'TLA' spread through both industry and academia, and it has now become a generally understood initialism."

> From Wikipedia:
> http://en.wikipedia.org/wiki/Three-letter_acronym

What we will start with first is the "C" word: Commission. Every sales rep you will talk with at a major company will be working on a commission basis at anywhere from 35-80% of their overall compensation. The software sales professional who comes to your office is paid a base salary, meaning the salary he/she receives no matter if they sell anything or not, plus a percentage of every sale made as an incentive to performance...the commission. Living off of a commission plan is hard for many. Learning how to budget for the highs and lows can be difficult. Every month I have a manager who looks at what I have done, what I have forecasted for the next month, and, depending upon my performance within those sixty days, will determine whether or not I need to be put on a "plan." A "plan" for a salesperson is like being put on probation for other employees. You have to start turning things around or you will need to "find suitable employment elsewhere." If you were looking for job security and something that didn't require a lifetime supply of TUMS® then you should be finding suitable employment elsewhere.

Our Common Sales Vocabulary - Not meant to be, by any means, an exhaustive dictionary, but enough to give you a good basic background

Account brief – a synopsis of the current opportunity for a given organization. Will contain a complete outline of the opportunity matching the terms of the sales process the company employs.

Caps – the other side to pricing discount penalties are caps. Companies will limit the amount of commission that could be paid on any given deal. For example, if your quota is $1,000,000 and some crazy huge deal comes in that is for $4,000,000, the company could have a policy that says it is not going to pay you for selling more than $2,000,000 in revenue in any given year. It's a company hedge against large commissions breaking the bank and I have been told by people before that believe it is also a fairness question. Any deal that big has multiple players in it doing yeomen's work without commission and over and above a certain value it has to be for the benefit of the company.

Change management – the ability to understand how the purchase that you are embarking upon is going to alter the as-is business processes of your organization and how best to optimize for the new system.

Champion – Every sales rep wants to develop their own champion within an organization that, eventually, becomes a person selling for the vendor internally.

Claw back – If you, as a customer, return a product every comp plan out there gives the company the right to "claw back" out of your future earnings the amount of the commissions that were paid to you. The moral of the story: sell good deals you are sure the customer is going to be happy with for a long time. You can't always predict everything and situations do happen, so about every salesperson I know has had a claw back or two in his career. Rarely have I seen large ones, but they do exist as cautionary tales to the younger sales reps just getting their feet wet in our wonderful world.

Closing – the process of actually bringing the sale to finality. It is generally used to mean final achievement of having the customer sign on the dotted line and deliver a check to the vendor. A salesperson may say, "I closed that sale," for example. There are many techniques taught for closing a deal. During a sales process you will, undoubtedly, have several "closing" steps utilized on you over time to gauge where you are with regard to your buying process. Each step towards closure is, in the sales rep's eyes, making the final "yes" an assumed and easy decision for the organization.

Coin-operated – The term refers to the fact that a sales rep will base his/her actions around how they are paid. If they are incented to sell one product over another in their compensation plan then they will, management hopes, sell that product over others. Put a coin into the machine, push a button, and a specific result should occur. I'm not a fan of this term because it means my sole motivation is money. It is that way for some, but not for me. Hopefully it isn't the only motivation for your sales rep either.

Commission – The amount paid to a sales rep based upon the compensation plan. These plans usually pay an elevating set of percentages of a sale based upon where they are towards their overall quota. It's like a sports athlete who is playing in a contract year. If I can sell just a little bit more on one sale it may get me to that next level of percentages which will then mean that the next sale is like hitting pay-dirt in the free agent market. Another common incentive is the quarterly bonus, which is a bonus based upon attaining a certain sales amount in a quarter. The intent is to help even out the sales so the company doesn't see a spike and drop in their sales every quarter, but can forecast a steady revenue stream. More than one sales rep I have known has postponed a sale into another quarter versus a current quarter because they either already had that bonus made or had no shot at it and wanted to make sure they gave themselves the opportunity to get the bonus in the next quarter. It shouldn't happen of course and if you are in control of the process it won't happen. Thank goodness.

Competitor battlecard – Marketing departments will create comparison cards that detail the differences between one company's products and another company's products. These cards will include specific language on how to win against the other company during a sale.

Consequence and value probes – Sales reps will use probing questions to seek out the answer to either what bad will happen if the organization does nothing or what good can happen if the organization moves forward with a sale. Either way, the goal of these probing questions is to understand if the organization has a committed understanding as to why they need to seal a deal.

Critical Business Issue (CBI) – It is an issue to be solved without which an organization cannot operate or remain viable in a business process. If a critical business function is interrupted, an organization could suffer serious financial, legal, or other damages to its mission.

Decision analysis – The part of the brief which deals with how the sales rep believes the actual sale with the organization can come to a decision. This isn't in regard to the particular needs and pains anymore, but rather deals with the nuts and bolts of a contract, the legal negotiations, and payments in order to know how all of that needs to gets done at that organization.

Decision maker – The person or group of people who can literally put their name on your contract for you. There are many kinds of decision makers in an organization, but only one or two can actually sign the contract to finalize the sale. It isn't always the executive director or CFO. That person is who every salesperson tries to identify early on because it could be different for every type of sale.

Demo – The part of the sales process where the vendor showcases the product for the potential client. This could be done in person or over the web, but is generally done in a manner that personalizes the product to the unique needs and pains of your organization.

Forecast – See *pipeline*.

Funnel – A graphical representation of the sales process from entry to final sale closure.

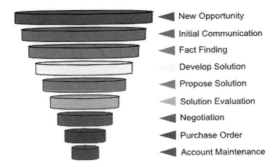

Gatekeeper – The person at a potential client who keeps guard over who a sales rep should or should not talk to. They control access with either positive or negative consequences depending upon how they manage their role.

Hard ROI – A return on investment (ROI) formula that deals with tangible costs of items, like equipment, computers, etc.

Hunter/gatherer – In sales teams you have different needs for selling to current customers as opposed to sales to new customers. As such the sales team is usually divided into at least a couple of different groups. These could be inside sales, outside field-based sales reps, or a mix. Whatever the mix it doesn't really make any difference to me. The hunter sales reps are focused on new business to the company no matter how they sell, face to face or over the phone for example. The gatherer sales reps are generally someone who deals with current customers selling upgrades, new services engagements, yearly maintenance and support and the like. Smaller vendors will sometimes put the gatherer sales positions under the marketing department where they can have one person fulfill a couple of different roles, i.e., lead generation and customer add-on sales. The gatherer reps make less commission than hunter reps as they are selling into defined customer sets and are able to close more sales more quickly than their hunter counterparts. Hunter sales are generally larger, take longer to bring in, and involve a great deal more company resources to manage. Each sales type requires a specific type of personality. Neither one is better than the other one is, and both are necessary to take care of customers during all points of relationship contact.

Interest generation statement – A specific set of tested verbiage designed to elicit an interest response from a potential client.

Key player profiles – These will be personality and job-related profiles of the organization's people involved in the sales process. This can be cursory for some folks and incredibly detailed for others all the way down to the types of knick-knacks on their desk, where they went to school, what part of town they live in, or what sports teams they like. Any information gathered is included here for potential useful reference by others at the vendor who will be jumping into help with parts of the sales process, but haven't had the benefit of the direct connection with the client.

Lead generation team – This I am going to lump into one common group for you. There are multiple ways you may come to know a vendor, and we have discussed the most common types. From the point you move from a target of a vendor to a possible lead, and then to a qualified prospect, you may actually touch several parts of the company. Whether you talked with someone at a tradeshow, called in off of a mailer, saw a product review online and filled out a form, or even attended a marketing webinar or seminar you could have talked to one to four people possibly by the time you are put into contact with the actual sales rep. At that point you are now the coveted "qualified lead!"

Needs identification – The process by the vendor of gathering the various needs and pains of an organization into a rational set of issues that you, as a vendor, can solve.

Opportunity – What an organization is called in a sales process with a vendor. The opportunity is the overall classification for all of the tasks, events, notes, and actions that occur within the sales process for that individual sale. One organization could have several "opportunities" assigned to it if the vendor is actively selling more than one product/solution at a time to that organization.

Pipeline – A list of the sales prospects that a sales rep is working on, ordered by the anticipated close date. May also be called a *forecast*.

Pricing discount penalties – Many companies will cut the commission percentages paid out should the discount on a sale reach over specific levels. It's a hedge to keep the sales team from discounting too heavily and using price to sell over and above a value equation.

Proof of concept – When a vendor, either through a paid engagement or as part of a free trial sales step, allows the potential client to test drive the software towards a specific set of goals that, if achieved, will decide a yes or no on a sale.

Prospect – Before you can be a client you are a prospect. Just like the old mining days, sales reps are "prospecting" for "gold" (the sale). You are the gold and thus the prospect. Some marketers like to add another category called suspect and define those as just names on a list that become prospects once they enter an actual sales process. This is just semantics as far as I'm concerned.

Quota – The amount of whatever product or services that the company wants you as the salesperson to sell. It is the end all and be all of being in sales. Every job a salesperson ever applies for will entail the question of how he/she performed as to quota in his/her previous job. Sales is a performance-based job easily tracked with tangible results. One VP of Sales I had once said, so wryly, that making 98% of quota means that you didn't make quota. Never liked that one much, but he was right. That 2% could make the difference between having a job and not having a job unfortunately. Not always fun, but it is the reality in sales positions.

Quota credit – It is actually possible for a sales rep to sell something and not get paid. Quota credit means that maybe another rep sold it or it was sold by a partner and the sales rep gets quota credit that helps them towards the next level of percentage payouts.

Recommendation – Gaining a recommendation from a trusted source to the organization goes a long way to becoming a trusted advisor yourself.

Rapport – A sales manager will always ask a rep who in the organization he/she has the best ability to speak openly and honestly with about the internal decision dynamics of the current sale. Hopefully this person will be able to become the champion.

Reference story – Being able to use reference stories are a great selling tool to show a potential client that others, just like them, have already made the decision to purchase the software that they are now considering.

Sales call script – The defined calling scripts companies use during a phone conversation to lead a prospect through specific qualifying questions. Based on these qualifiers, a sales rep will make an initial decision as to whether or not an organization is a right fit for the vendor's products.

Sales manager – This person is either a sales team leader only or, in a small company, could also hold an executive title and have to do more than only manage a sales team. Sales teams are usually fairly small, no more than ten reps per manager. That is based on the axiom that if a sales manager spends one hour a day doing the weekly one-on-one meetings he/she could easily have two out of every five workdays be only those meetings. The sales manager has the main job of ensuring the sales reps' activities are positively moving qualified prospects through the sales process, to make sure the salesperson is getting the proper support throughout the rest of the company when needed, and to be the personnel overseer for all things needed (rote tasks of vacation time management, expense reports, etc). The sales manager also has the unenviable task of reporting to management his/her sales team's activity or lack thereof. It is a tough position because he/she is responsible for sales numbers without having had any real direct impact on creating. Many former salespeople believe they would like to be in management and then decide, once there, they would rather be in sales because, as managers, they can't control their own destiny. It is the definition of a middle management job where you are squeezed from above and below. Sales managers are paid a base salary plus, generally, a bonus structure based on the quota attainment of their team, equal to probably about 30 or 40% of their overall compensation. I admire, with great fondness, the really good sales managers I have had over the years and generally just try to work around the bad ones in order to make my goals. The good ones help me, as a sales rep, be successful in my job while the bad ones are just a barrier. For both the good and the bad ones I have sympathy because I don't think I want that job at most companies.

Sales representative – This person is supposed to be your main point of contact, your advocate at the organization during and, possibly, after the sales process. Their job is to be the quarterback of the team, the conductor of the orchestra, or, as I like to joke, the puppet master trying to make sure that the marionettes on the strings do everything I need them to do. They usually have roughly 50% of their income from commissions. Obviously, getting the sale is very important to this person and he/she is incentivized to work for you. Sales reps carry competing goals in their job. They want to do the best they can to help the customer be able to purchase their product, but also have to keep the company's goals in mind. If the customer's ability to purchase in a certain way is in conflict with the company goals it can be an uncomfortable situation.

Services/Implementation/Training/Consulting team – These team members are brought in once the qualified prospect has reached the stage that there is an imminent project or pending sale. They do not appreciate being brought in too early in the process and for good reason. If the technical salesperson and I haven't fully outlined the critical business issues, don't have the pricing aspects qualified, and don't know when a particular project needs to be sold and then completed, I am just wasting their time. Their work requires a good deal of time with an attention to detail that is vitally important because they are putting together the documents the implementation team will use to carry out their work. If you are not involved in some serious and long discussions with this group before you sign on the dotted line for an implementation of a business software application then you should STOP what you are about to do and ask to have those discussions. If you are being sold some sort of "standardized methodology" or "quick start" package at a special bundled price, be very careful. Services delivery is very specialized and this is one area, like training, you really get what you pay for and that may not be a good thing. The pain of a new implementation on a staff is not worth cutting corners when it comes to the services and training for implementation.

Soft ROI – A return on investment formula that deals on a value-based scenario for soft costs, such as employee time, productivity, and the like.

Solution selling – A sales training technique that teaches a value-based approach to working with potential clients, addressing pains, and creating solutions instead of just selling products.

Stay to get paid – Companies almost always write into their sales comp agreements that you only get paid if you are an active employee of the company. If you leave the company you generally forfeit any commissions still owed you. This is generally perplexing to me. I figure if the sales rep has earned it, then pay him/her and be done with it, but the rule is there, and has always been explained to me, as a way to keep the sales reps from closing the big deal and then running off to another company without sticking around to make sure the deal they have sold is successful. I appreciate that, but I've seen remote reps do nothing but play general contractor on their house and do practically nothing on the new sales front after the big paycheck, waiting till the claw back clause is out of effect before they can quit for that next big job. I have not done that, but distinctly remember calling a few friends and hearing nothing but construction for months while they did the minimal work to keep their job until the commissions were safe. This policy is also in effect if someone is terminated with cause. If that happens you aren't going to be getting paid. Sorry.

Subject matter experts – Vendors will have people on their staff who are experts in certain specific areas of the business processes that they attempt to solve. These subject matter experts (SMEs) will be brought in at points in a sales process to help get over what are expected difficult spots of understanding. Their goal is to make a difficult section of the sales process simpler to get through by making some part of the product/solution easier to understand and applicable to a customer's needs. An invaluable resource to a sales rep when used properly.

Success kit – A set of sales tools arranged for certain market segments that showcase the strengths of the company's products to those customers.

Stakeholder – Someone at the organization who has a direct and vested interest in the success of the project being proposed.

Technical salesperson – There are a number of different titles this person may hold, but the gist is this person is the technical expert brought in to walk you through product demonstrations, create proof-of-concept demos, and explain the arduous details of a product in a way that is quick and easy. The training and technical expertise these folks have in order to be good at their jobs is extensive. In many ways they are as good as the implementation services people you may meet, but choose to work on the sales side of the house.

They also usually work on a base salary plus a commission percentage that is around 15-30% of their overall compensation. The common mistake for a client to make is to talk to these folks like they are regular tech folks and not as part of the sales team that they are. I've learned so much from customers having technical discussions with one of my technical salespeople not really even realizing all of the questions they are asking are going into the overall equation to try to make the deal close. A technical sales team manager I knew back in the late 90s called the technical sales team the "wolves in sheep's clothing." He meant that many times in the sales process customers will feel more comfortable telling information to or asking certain questions of technical salespeople for the sheer fact they are not the "salesperson."

Territory – The geographic area where a sales rep is assigned to sell for the vendor. Geography is the general principle for laying out a territory for a rep, but sometimes other criteria are used such as vertical markets (higher education, healthcare, K-12, government, faith-based, etc.).

User and technical decisions – Before an actual contract is signed, sales processes talk of winning two parts of the sale: the user decision and technical decision. Sometimes the users choose one product while the technical people at the organization choose another for whatever reason. Depending upon the organization, one or the other group will hold sway over what the final decision makers will choose. Depending upon the product being sold, the users or the technical group may hold greater sway than the other for other types of sales. Your sales rep will know which group their product plays best to and will try to neutralize one group while making champions out of the others.

Vice president of sales – Ah, the big gun. The executive who swoops in to talk at a high level to your high level folks and give everyone that warm fuzzy feeling. I tease, but they can be very helpful. People like feeling special by having company bigwigs pay attention to them. The vice president reports to either the CEO or to an executive vice president if there are multiple divisions in the company (multiple company operations, product lines, etc.). As you might imagine, seeing the trend here, the VP of sales has a good portion of his/her compensation based upon a rollup of the sales of the teams that are directly under his/her control. Those sales numbers the sales department executives must commit to and report on are everything to them. They are solely judged on making these numbers and are held personally accountable if their teams do not make them. As awful as it sounds, almost every quarter I have been in a sales position I have been asked to provide a forecast number to my boss that states what number I would guarantee to bring in, sign in blood as it were, what I hope I can bring in, and what is a long shot. Those numbers go into a manager's report which is then collated into a VP of sales report that has to then be reported to the full executive team of the company. Decisions about hiring in all departments of the company, benefits that are added or deleted, and other major company decisions are all based upon the sales projections that start from my sales desk. No pressure, right?

Do you feel like you just learned a little sales lingo? Excellent!

**Sample Sales Compensation Document
(Names and dates removed to protect the innocent)**

Though lengthy and complex in its legal language, I believe this is important to see in order to see how a vendor would generally like to manage a sales representative. This document for sales compensation plan is fairly common and contains many standard concepts the vast majority of sales reps out there will recognize.

As I've mentioned elsewhere, I would encourage you to have the compensation discussion with your sales reps to understand how they are paid to see if there is a way their comp plan can be utilized to your advantage within your own buying process. You never know. It might help.

My comments on each section are noted. Look for the words in bold **'AU COMMENT'**.

20XX Company A Sales Compensation Plan
Personal Plan Summary For Andrew Urban

[AU COMMENT - Sales reps are always paid a commission on a percentage of the sale. Younger and more startup companies will typically pay higher percentages as a way to incent sales reps at a company where sales are hard to come by due to lack of name recognition or other factors. More mature companies will pay percentages usually 50-75% less than startup companies, but the sales are easier to come by with a mature company than at the start up or smaller company.]
Commissions Based Compensation

Software and Services Revenue* Commissions Rates Base Rate (0-100% of Quota and Qualified Renewals and Upsells (see Ts&Cs)) 5.5%
Accelerator Rate 1
(100-125% of Quota – Non renewals) 8.0%

Accelerator Rate 1
(greater than 125% of Quota – Non renewals).............................10.0%

[AU COMMENT - Less money is always paid for renewal sales than new sales. New sales are just plain harder to bring in the door than renewal sales.]
Product A Renewal Rate.......... 3.75%
Product B New Sales Rate**... 5.625%

Plan Period: January 1, 20XX – December 31, 20XX (new plan to take effect thereafter)

[AU COMMENT - There is always a quota amount that is expected and here it is for that year. Make your number. If not, there had better either be business conditions as to why not or you had better be looking for alternate employment.]
Software and Services Revenue Objectives:
"20XX Yearly Quota" $1.5 million

Quota Credit earned for:
- Product A New Sales
- Product A Renewals
- Product B New Sales (No renewals)

[AU COMMENT - A commission split happens when two or more sales reps have material involvement in a sale.]
** Commission splitting applicable to Product B
New Sales--additional 3.75% to be paid to (TBD)
(Product B New Sales will count toward quota, but no Accelerator Rates are applied to Product B Sales unless specified).

[AU COMMENT - And now the inevitable legalese rears its ugly head. Here we go!]
All compensation hereunder subject to the more detailed Terms and Conditions attached hereto.

20XX Company A SALES COMPENSATION PLAN
Terms and Conditions

[AU COMMENT - The first sections are legal ways to say that the plan only covers certain things during a certain time period and nothing else end of story.]

1.0 Plan Scope

These are the terms and conditions of the 20XX Company A Sales Compensation Plan (the "Plan") for Qualified Accepted contracts (as defined in Section 3.2.1 below, the "QA Contracts") in fiscal year 20XX. Our goal is to provide a compensation plan that is achievable, clear and understandable, easy to administer, and provides an environment that enables you to excel. This plan is designed to support Company A's objectives and reward you accordingly for your efforts and results. References to Company A or the Company within the Plan are references to Company A, Inc.

1.1 Plan Components

The Plan consists of (1) these Terms and Conditions and (2) an individualized, job-specific, compensation plan (the "Personal Plan Summary" or "PPS"), which sets forth the specific compensation and compensation calculations that are applicable to the Plan Participant.

1.2 Plan Term

The Plan covers QA Contracts during the 20XX Fiscal Year (January 1, 20XX through December 31, 20XX, the "Plan Period") including without limitation, those contracts that may have been accepted prior to the introduction of this Plan in 20XX. This Plan shall not be modified in any way unless authorized in writing by the Chief Operating Officer (the "COO"). The 20XX Company A Corporate Sales Compensation Plan expired by its terms on December 31, 20XX (a confirmation of this termination was emailed on December 28, 20XX which also gave notice of this Plan's introduction) and does not apply to any sales made in 20XX. Any commissions or credits from prior plan years will be subject to the terms and conditions of the commission's plan or policy in effect at the time the particular transaction was completed. No compensation shall be paid on any contract under this Plan for the Plan Period unless such contract is a QA Contract. This Plan terminates on December 31, 20XX and shall not apply to any sales or contracts entered into following the Plan Period and will be replaced by a separate and new plan to be announced by the Senior Vice President, Sales ("SVP of Sales") and COO. Although the new plan for Fiscal Year 20XX may not be announced until after the beginning of Fiscal Year 20XX, its terms shall apply to all contracts Accepted from January 1, 20XX and thereafter.

[AU COMMENT - I guess I have to be an employee to earn commission. Who'd a thunk it!]

1.3 Plan Eligibility

The terms and conditions of the Plan are applicable to all full-time salespersonnel employed by Company A who are assigned a PPS (defined below) to which these Terms and Conditions are attached ("Eligible Employees"). Each Eligible Employee will be given a copy of the Plan.

2.0 Compensation

Your compensation may include any or all of the following Plan features: Base Salary and Variable Compensation (which may consist of commissions, bonus or a combination of commissions and bonus). Individual plan features will be included on a Plan Participant's respective PPS.

[AU COMMENT - A base salary for an outside field sales rep is generally 40-60% of his/her overall compensation plan. This is intended to make sure that the rep reaches for the commissions and doesn't get too comfortable on the base salary. The vendor wants the sales rep a little bit comfortable to keep the loyalty factor high and a little bit hungry to make sure the rep goes after the new business necessary.]

2.1 Base Salary

Plan Participants shall earn the Base Salary which may be amended from time to time with prior written notice and maintained in the records of the Company's payroll department. The Base Salary will vary according to job title, experience, and/or position.

2.2 Variable Compensation

Variable Compensation may consist of commissions, bonus or a combination of commissions and bonus as specifically set forth in a Plan Participant's PPS.

2.2.1 Commissions Compensation

Commissions compensation is unique to each position and is paid for the two major components of Company A sales revenue: (a) sales of Software and Services and (b) transaction or donations processed. Two distinct sets of commission rates may apply (if at all) to each component as specifically set forth in your PPS.

[AU COMMENT - Another legal mind twist....if I'm not involved in the sale I don't get paid. So I have to be on staff and involved in order to get paid. Got it. When a company tries to outsmart itself commissions are frequently miscalculated. I always like the compensation plans that say, "Sell this and get paid this." Not very hard to figure out, but too easy I guess since no one ends up doing that.]

2.2.1.1 Software and Services Revenue Commissions

Software and Services Revenue Commissions will be paid to Plan Participants only if specifically provided for in the Plan Participant's PPS and are based on a percentage of the recognized and collected value of a QA Contract. Sales commission percentages shall be established by management and are specifically set forth in each PPS. In certain cases, accelerator commission rates may apply if defined quotas/goals (as specifically set forth in the PPS) are met; the terms of that acceleration must be set forth in the PPS to be applicable to a Plan Participant.

Conditions for earning Software and Services Revenue Commissions are stated below. The Company will distribute a regular commission statement (the "Commissions Statement") to the Plan Participant that describes all paid commission payments, including without limitation Transaction Revenue Commissions, (and offsets) made to the Plan Participant for that period. It is the responsibility of the Plan Participant to report any errors on a commission statement within thirty (30) days of the date of the statement. Requests for adjustments to commissions must be communicated in writing to the Sales Manager and the SVP of Sales with a copy to legal@companya.com. If, after consideration by the SVP of Sales, an adjustment is deemed necessary, the SVP will submit this determination to the COO for final written approval. Following final approval by the COO, that adjustment will be set forth in writing on a monthly commission statement within 60 days following the reported error.

2.2.2 Bonus Based Compensation

Bonus payments will be paid to Plan Participants only if specifically provided for in the Plan Participant's PPS and may be made for the achievement of certain quotas, targets or a percentage or combination thereof attributable to Plan Participant or a group reporting to a Plan Participant or some portion (or all) of the Company's Quota or other target, all as may be specifically set forth in the PPS. Bonuses are offered to reward long-term productivity and encourage continued employment. The bonus is earned as the payments are received and recognized for the credited Quota amount on which the bonus was based; however, the Company may elect to pay the bonuses prior to being earned discussed below in Section 3.3.3, but only if the Plan Participant is employed by Company A on the date the bonus is scheduled for payment.

3.0 Plan Administration

[AU COMMENT - Now that we've said what you could earn we let you know that it is all up to the Senior VP of Sales and

COO to decide if the deal you sell is qualified enough to allow you to be paid on it.]

3.1 Plan Management

The SVP of Sales and COO shall make the final and binding determination of any amount payable under the Plan and reserves the right to adjust, modify or change the Plan at any time before a commission or bonus is earned, either during or after the close of the Plan Period. Commissions and bonuses are not earned until the Company makes any and all final determinations and adjustments, modifications or changes as authorized by the Plan. Adjustments, modifications, and changes may be made to bonuses, commissions, commission rates, quotas, territories, splits or any other terms and conditions and may result in a decrease or an increase in compensation. In addition, these Terms and Conditions are subject to revision at any time. Notification of any revisions to these Terms and Conditions will be via electronic mail or in hard copy or in such other reasonable manner as management may elect.

3.2 QA Criteria; Quota Credit

[AU COMMENT - Notice the words "Qualified" and "Accepted." This is pretty normal, especially now in the days of Sarbanes Oxley legislation that strictly regulates revenue recognition by software firms. Software firms have very specific rules by which they can recognize revenue that is sold and what contract terms they can or cannot accept.]

3.2.1 Qualified Accepted Contracts Compensation will only be earned under this Plan on contracts that are Qualified and Accepted during the Plan Period.

A contract is "Qualified" only if such contract:
• calls for software subscription, implementation and/or professional services (setup, activation, training), data and/or screening services, creative or integration services, strategic consulting service and/or leads to transaction revenue; and
• has been procured in compliance with all applicable laws, all Company A policies applicable to the sale and marketing of

Company A products and services, and all procedures and policies referred to herein and as then in effect; and
• is not subject to any written or oral "side" agreements or terms; and
• if for the sale of implementation services, such services are scheduled to commence no later than six (6) months from the time of Acceptance; and
• if for the sale of consulting services, such services are scheduled to commence no later than three (3) months from the time of Acceptance.

The SVP of Sales and Director of Corporate Sales shall send monthly reports to the COO setting forth a list of actual and potential Qualified Renewals assigned to Plan Participants.

[AU COMMENT - Have to define what is a new sale versus a renewal sale.]
A contract is classified as a "renewal" if the customer was previously a customer of Company A (or channel/referral/etc., as the case may be) within the 12 months preceding the date the contract is signed.

The "Qualified Upsell Revenues" with regard to a renewal contract shall be equal to the Value of such contract less the "Base Renewal Rate" (which shall be equal to the revenues to Company A associated with such customer's previous contract plus any addenda thereto).

A contract is "Accepted" only after it is duly executed by Company A's Chief Financial Officer and an appropriate representative of the customer with the power and authority to so bind the customer after having received the necessary approvals therefor.

[AU COMMENT - Even after a contract is accepted and qualified it can later become unaccepted and unqualified!]
A contract initially deemed an Accepted Qualified Contract may be subsequently rejected (in whole or in part) by the CFO or the COO if:

- within 12 months of Acceptance, it is discovered that the contract did not meet all of the criteria for a Qualified contract as set forth above; or
- within 12 months of Acceptance, the contract is substantially scaled back or cancelled by either party (including any partner or reseller). Substantially scaled back means a reduction or refund in the original Accepted contract value of 10% or more (a "Scale Back").

[AU COMMENT - If a contract is scaled back during the term then the company can still come back and reduce or take back paid commissions. This is the incentive from the company for the sales rep to try not to oversell a product, sell a product incorrectly, and encourage the rep to aid in communications after the sale to ensure a successful transition to implementation.]

3.2.2 Quota Crediting

Plan Participants will receive credit toward their 20XX Yearly Quota (or target amounts, as the case may be) based on the Value of Qualified Accepted Contracts which have not been rejected, to the extent permitted and specifically set forth in the Plan Participant's PPS)

3.3   Payment Terms – Variable Compensation

[AU COMMENT - Once again I have to be employed by the company to receive commission. Goodness.]

3.3.1 Software and Services Revenue Commissions

Software and Services Revenue Commission on QA Contracts are earned only while the Plan Participant is employed by Company A and only to the extent the following four conditions are met within the first 12 months of the contract:

(1) the Company recognizes the revenue under the QA Contract;
(2) the Company receives payment of all invoice(s) under the QA Contract;
(3) the QA Contract is not Scaled Back; and

(4) the customer (or the channel/reseller as the case may be) not cancel the contract or default on payments under the contract.

[AU COMMENT - This is fun because the recognition of the contract itself could potentially take longer than the 12 months described. I have seen other employers unscrupulously use rules like this to string out paying commissions for as long as possible. This makes for a very unhappy sales rep. Maybe ask your sales rep how long they have been at their company as well as how long they have been in their current position. That could tell you whether or not reps move in or out or around the company because of yearly changing compensation plans.]

Plan Participants will not earn 100% of eligible commissions on a QA Contract until the sale relating to the first 12 months of such contract has been fully recognized, pursuant to Company A's revenue recognition guidelines, and Company A receives all payments from the customer (or the channel/reseller as the case may be) due under the QA Contract for such period. Plan Participants are compensated both for procuring QA Contracts (and Upsells and channel/referral partners as the case may be) and collections. Thus, Plan Participants must not only initiate sales but also maintain and continue to service their accounts to ensure timely collection and satisfaction with the services provided.

[AU COMMENT - For this contract the rep is scheduled to be paid within a month after the sale is completed, accepted, and deemed qualified. It may take a few weeks to have a contract be finally accepted and so forth.]

Payment of the full estimated Software and Services Revenue Commission as determined by the QA Contract's Value will be paid to Plan Participants within 2 pay periods following the month in which the Company receives the customer's (or channel/reseller as the case may be) initial payment(s) under such contract, subject to the termination provisions set forth in Section 3.7. However, all commission payments will be reviewed and may be adjusted by management based upon the collections actually received by

Company A, customer defaults, amounts refunded, Scale Backs and order cancellations and other adjustments set forth herein within the first 12 months of the contract.

3.3.3   Bonus Payments

Plan Participants are eligible to receive bonuses if and as specifically set forth in their PPS subject to these Terms and Conditions. Plan Participants may, in the discretion of the COO, receive payment of estimated bonuses, subject to the termination provisions set forth in Section 3.7. prior to the Plan Participant fully earning such bonus. Bonuses are earned only while the Plan is in effect. Bonus payments shall be paid within two months following the end of each quarter.

[AU COMMENT - A sales rep is commonly called into help with Accounts Receivables that have lapsed out. This provision is in here to make it worth their while to help make sure the bills get paid to the vendor.]

3.4   Commission/Bonus/Quota Recovery

If a customer's (or channel/reseller as the case may be) accounts receivable becomes greater than ninety (90) days past due at any time during the first 12 months of the contract, all prior commission payments, or bonus credits/payments advanced to the employee based upon the unpaid amounts that are past due will be deducted from the employee's current commissions or bonuses, and his/her current Quota achievement credit may be adjusted; provided that such affected Plan Participant may appeal such adjustment within 30 days to the SVP of Sales and the COO (with a copy to legal@companya.com). The COO will determine the matter in his sole discretion based on the facts and circumstances of each individual situation. In some cases advanced commission or bonus reconciliations may cause a negative compensation balance. If this occurs, no commission or bonus payments will be made to Plan Participants until the entire negative balance has been offset in full with earned commissions and bonuses.

If an account is credit adjusted, or deemed uncollectable and written off under the terms of the Company's accounting policies, no prior commissions, quota credits or bonus credits associated with the sale will be repaid and quota credits will not be restored regardless of whether the account is paid at a later date.

[AU COMMENT - If you are in a sales negotiation and are angling for a big discount remember there might be an incentive for the rep to try to keep the price as high as possible.]

3.5   Pricing Discount Penalties

All product-pricing discounts and changes to the Company's standard form contract must be made in accordance with the current published pricing and discounting policies (as set forth in the pricing calculator) and the Finance practices then in effect. If a Plan Participant submits an order with an unapproved discount or contract terms, neither the Plan Participant nor that Plan Participant's manager will receive commission or bonus payment, or quota credit for that transaction.

3.6(a) Commission Splits

Commissions may not be split between or among any two individuals unless (1) specifically approved by the COO in his sole discretion (and the aggregate of any such approved split shall not exceed the aggregate amount of the commission payable if no such split had occurred) or (2) specifically permitted and set forth in such Plan Participant's PPS.

3.6(b) 20XX Yearly Quota

Sales plans are based upon an annual quota (any deviations will be reflected in the Plan Participant's PPS). Quotas for Plan Participants who are subject to a quota will be reflected in that individual Plan Participant's PPS.

[AU COMMENT - Sales plans always say that nothing in the agreement implies guaranteed employment and that you as the sales rep can be terminated at any time. This is one of the

standard provisions that spawns the "What have you done for me lately?" sales attitudes I've seen in many sales departments.]

3.7 Termination and Transfers

Plan Participant understands that this Plan does not guarantee employment for any definite term. Unless otherwise set forth in any written Employment Agreement signed by Company A's COO and Chief Executive Officer, either the Plan Participant or Company A may terminate the employment relationship at any time and for any reason with or without cause and with or without notice.

[AU COMMENT - If you quit you get nothing. That seems wrong to many who are new to sales since they feel that since they earned it they should be paid it no matter what, but this is the way it is with about every sales plan I've ever seen. If you aren't with the company don't expect to be paid.]

If a Plan Participant voluntarily resigns from Company A, transfers to another position within Company A, or is terminated, his/her ability to earn commissions and bonuses under the Plan terminates on his/her last date of employment with Company A or, where the Plan Participant is transferring to a different position, on the effective date of the transfer. Any compensation earned up to the date of resignation, termination or transfer will be paid to the Plan Participant, less any outstanding debts (commission recovery, advances outstanding, etc.). If the Plan Participant resigns or voluntarily transfers to another position, commissions will only be paid for sums collected from the customer up to the date of the Plan Participant's resignation or transfer. If the Plan Participant is involuntarily terminated or involuntarily transferred, Company A will pay the Plan Participant for commissions earned and collected from the customer up to the termination date and will additionally pay the Plan Participant for funds collected from the customer through the last day of the month following the effective date of the Plan Participant's termination or voluntary transfer. After such period has passed, no commissions will be paid based on customer collections for any reason.

[AU COMMENT - **If you voluntarily leave and have a negative commission balance they will deduct everything they can from your final check.**]

If an employee voluntarily resigns or is terminated with a negative compensation balance, the advanced but unearned amount of commissions and bonuses will be withheld from the final compensation owed to the employee under this Plan, with the exception of minimum wages due under state law. Where the employee's final wages are insufficient to cover the amount owing, the Plan Participant will be required to make payment directly to the Company within 30 days of being notified of the amount owing. In addition, a Plan Participant's salary or other compensation payments may be used to offset any negative compensation balance. No reconciliations of advanced commissions or bonuses already paid to a Plan Participant (i.e., no deductions or requests for re-payments) will be made or required after the effective date of the Plan Participant's termination or resignation.

[AU COMMENT - **Guess what? You have to pay taxes on your commissions. Commissions are actually taxed at a higher rate by the federal government than standard pay.**]

3.9 Withholding

All forms of compensation set forth in this Plan are subject to applicable withholdings, payroll taxes, and any other deductions required by law.

[AU COMMENT - **This is the classic part of every plan which says that no matter whatever else I said I can change the plan at any time to suit the needs of the company. The dreaded word "re-goal" is something no sales rep likes to here. "Re-goal" means that the company arbitrarily makes your quota higher because you have done too well too fast.**]

3.10 Amendment and Termination of Plan

Company A reserves and retains the right to modify, rescind or terminate this Plan in whole or in part, at any time during the Plan

Period, at its sole discretion, with prior notice to Plan Participants, and nothing in this Plan limits this right in any way or creates any rights in any Plan Participant of future participation in this Plan or any other Plan, or constitutes any guarantee of compensation or employment with the Company. Further, Company A does not have any obligation under this Plan or otherwise to adopt this or any other compensation plan in the future. Any modification to this Plan may only be made in a writing signed by the Company A's COO.

[AU COMMENT - Last legalese is always here for ethical standards, any potential need for arbitration, and other miscellaneous clauses and we're all done. I've left the legalese out here since it is enormous and isn't very relevant overall.]

3.11 Ethical and Legal Standards

[AU COMMENT - This section usually includes policies on gifts or entertainment, side agreements, violations of trade practices, and the penalties involved.]

3.12 Agreement to Arbitrate.

[AU COMMENT - insert any standard arbitration language here that you ever seen in other contracts and you have what would normally go here.]

3.13 Misc.

[AU COMMENT - insert any standard miscellaneous legalese here.]

[AU COMMENT - You can now negotiate a sales compensation plan. Congratulations!]

Notes

Chapter 2: The Nonprofit Buyer

1. http://www.tradingmarkets.com/news/stock-alert/blkb_blackbaud-reports-fourth-quarter-and-full-year-2009-results-776044.html
2. http://www.microsoft.com/msft/reports/ar09/10k_fh_fin.html

Chapter 3: Unreliable Buying Techniques

3. http://www.referenceforbusiness.com/biography/F-L/Kelleher-Herb-1931.html
4. J. Mike Jacka, Paulette J. Keller, *Business Process Mapping: Improving Customer Satisfaction, 2nd Edition* (John Wiley & Sons, July 2009).

Chapter 4: The Other Side of the Fence

5. http://www.brainyquote.com/quotes/quotes/p/peterdruck154447.html

Chapter 5: How a Sales Process Works on You

6. http://www.imdb.com/title/tt0104348/
7. http://www.imdb.com/title/tt0104348/
8. Keith Eades, *The New Solution Selling* (New York: McGraw-Hill, 2004).
9. William "Skip" Miller, *Proactive Selling* (New York: Amacom, 2003).

Made in the USA
Charleston, SC
08 October 2013